W9-BRC-619

AMC GUIDE TO

Mount Desert Island

AND

Acadia National Park

Also Available from
the Appalachian Mountain Club

AMC Trail Guides
Guide to Mt. Washington and the Presidential Range
Hiking the Mountain State (West Virginia)
Maine Mountain Guide
Massachusetts and Rhode Island Trail Guide
North Carolina Hiking Trails
Short Hikes and Ski Trips Around Pinkham Notch
White Mountain Guide

AMC River Guides
Maine
Massachusetts/Connecticut/Rhode Island
New Hampshire/Vermont

Trail Building and Maintenance
Robert D. Proudman and Reuben Rajala

Backcountry Facilities
Design and Maintenance
R.E. Leonard, E.L. Spencer, and H.J. Plumley

The Conservationworks Book
Lisa Capone

Organizing Outdoor Volunteers
Roger L. Moore, Vicki LaFarge, Charles L. Tracy

AMC Quiet Water Canoe Guides
New Hampshire/Vermont
Massachusetts/Connecticut/Rhode Island
Alex Wilson

AMC Guide to Winter Camping
Stephen Gorman

AMC GUIDE TO
Mount Desert Island
AND
Acadia National Park

Fifth edition

compiled by the Appalachian Mountain Club

field guide by Chris Elfring

illustrated by D.D. Tyler

map by Patrick Dunlavey

APPALACHIAN MOUNTAIN CLUB BOOKS
BOSTON, MASSACHUSETTS

Cover Photo: Tammis Coffin
Book Design: Carol Bast Tyler
Illustrations © 1992 Diana Dee Tyler, except Harbor Porpoise on
  p. 71, © 1977.

Copyright © 1993 Appalachian Mountain Club. All rights reserved.
Distributed by The Talman Company

Published by the Appalachian Mountain Club. No part of this publication may
be reproduced or transmitted in any form or by any means, electronic or
mechanical, including photocopying and recording, or by any information
storage or retrieval system, except as may be expressly permitted by the 1976
Copyright Act or in writing from the Publisher. Requests for permission
should be addressed in writing to Appalachian Mountain Club Books, 5 Joy
St., Boston, MA 02108.

Library of Congress Cataloging-in-Publication Data

AMC guide to Mount Desert Island and Acadia National Park / compiled
  by the Appalachian Mountain Club: field guide by Chris Elfring;
  illustrated by D.D. Tyler; map by Patrick Dunlavey.—5th ed.
      p. cm.
    Map inserted in pocket.
    Inludes index.
    ISBN 1-878239-22-8: $10.95
    1. Hiking—Maine—Mount Desert Island—Guidebooks. 2. Hiking—
Maine—Acadia National Park—Guidebooks. 3. Mount Desert Island
(Me.)—Guidebooks. 4. Acadia National Park (Me.)—Guidebooks.
I. Elfring, Chris. II. Appalachian Mountain Club.
GV199.42.M22M683   1993
796.5'2'0974145—dc20   92-47221
                                                                  CIP

The paper used in this publication meets the minimum requirements of the
American National Standard for Information Sciences—Permanence of Paper
for Printed Library Materials, ANSI Z39.48–1984.∞

**Due to changes in conditions,
use of the information in this book
is at the sole risk of the user.**

♲ Printed on recycled paper.

Printed in the United States of America.

10 9 8 7 6 5 4 3 2 1   93 94 95 96 97

Contents

Introduction   vii

Section One: History   1

Section Two: Nature   14
    Plant Life   14
    Animal Life   38
    Ocean Life   61

Section Three: Trails   73
    Eastern District   77
    Western District   113
    Western Mountains   121
    Isle au Haut   127

Appendix A: Exploring   135
  Mount Desert Island

Appendix B: Sources For More Information   138

Index A: Trails   139

Index B: Nature   143

About the Appalachian Mountain Club   147

Introduction

THE APPALACHIAN MOUNTAIN CLUB has produced this guidebook in the hope that it will help you to enjoy and protect one of America's most beautiful natural resources: Mount Desert Island (MDI) and Acadia National Park. In these pages you will find out about Acadia's history and its wildlife. You will also find detailed descriptions of the hiking trails on Mount Desert Island and Acadia's other large island, Isle au Haut.

This expanded edition of the guidebook is one component of a new Appalachian Mountain Club/Acadia National Park partnership. We have teamed up to share expertise in trail building and land protection, environmental education, and volunteerism. By pooling our resources and working with other organizations, most notably Friends of Acadia, we will be better able to promote awareness of the park's natural resources and protect them for future visitors.

Coming to know Acadia National Park could well consume a lifetime, yet most visitors have only a few days. It is possible, however, to transform an ordinary visit into a journey of discovery. All it takes is a willingness to explore. This guide can help you in your journey. It can help you find your way along the island's 120 miles of maintained hiking trails, help you hike safely and comfortably, and help you better understand the environment and history of Mt. Desert Island. But more important than any guide is you—your sense of adventure. Be sure to bring it along.

Before You Go

Before you set out on your explorations, please remember these guidelines for safe hiking:

- Select a hiking route reasonable for you and your companions. A useful rule-of-thumb is to select a hike that is within the abilities of the least experienced person in your group.

- The trail descriptions in Section 3 include the National Park Service's level-of-difficulty ratings for each trail. These can serve as a general guide of a trail's difficulty; more can be learned by reading the trail descriptions themselves.

- Think about how long your hike will take and when the sun will set so you can return to your starting point before dark.

- Check the weather report before you go. The park service posts daily weather forecasts at the Hulls Cove Visitor Center.

- Carry a daypack—a small backpack with adjustable, padded shoulder straps and perhaps a waist belt. Make sure the compartment is large enough to contain the following: plenty of water in shatterproof bottles (one quart per person), lunch and high-energy snacks for the trail, map and guidebook, pocket knife, rain gear and extra clothing, sunglasses, a small first-aid kit, and perhaps a camera, sketchbook, or other personal items.

- Your clothing should be loose-fitting, flexible, and versatile. In the summer most Acadia hikers seem to wear cotton T-shirts and shorts, but cotton absorbs moisture and so can give you a chill if you perspire or get caught in the rain. A wool sweater is useful—wool stays warm even when wet. Synthetic fabrics that "breathe" such as polypropylene are good because they won't absorb moisture. Many experienced hikers carry a combination of natural and synthetic fabrics so they can layer their clothing according to conditions.

- Wear hiking boots. Low sneakers, running shoes, or street shoes just don't provide enough support for your feet and ankles on the rocky and uneven surfaces of woodland trails. They also become slippery in wet weather. There are many different types of lightweight, reasonably priced hiking boots available.

- Although Acadia National Park is relatively small, it is still possible to get lost. If you and your partners can't seem to orient yourself with the map or guidebook, stop and relax. Look around you to identify landmarks, such as a stream. If you are certain that you passed a trail junction or another familiar place within the last few minutes, retrace your steps to it and try to orient yourself from there. If you are still lost after trying these measures, stay where you are. Never leave the trail. Someone will find you, and it's much easier to do so if you are on the trail.

- If you are hiking with children, make sure they are well equipped, too. Children old enough to hike should be prepared just as adults, with proper footwear, clothing, water, and food. Match your hike to the children's abilities—there are many relatively easy trails within the park appropriate for family hikes.

Protecting Acadia National Park

Protecting and preserving Acadia National Park for future generations is everyone's responsibility. In that spirit the AMC and the National Park Service urges all visitors to follow these simple guidelines.

- Don't litter. Let "carry in–carry out" be your guide on the trail. Carry out everything you bring with you. Please pack out any trash you find along the trail, too— you will help make others' experience more enjoyable.

- Protect forest plants by staying on the trails. Use bridges, rocks, or logs designated to assist hikers through bogs or over tough spots on the trail. Don't bushwhack.

- Please do not disturb cairns, signs, bog bridges, and other trail markers and aids.

- Please refrain from smoking in the park during periods of high fire danger.

- Please do not pick flowers or take other plant samples. Take photographs as souvenirs instead. Blueberries and other fruit may be picked for personal consumption.

- Camp only in campgrounds. Camping on trails is prohibited throughout the park.

- Fires are permitted only in designated firepits in campgrounds and picnic areas.

- Pets on leashes no longer than six feet are allowed everywhere in the park except on Sand Beach, Echo Lake Beach, and on hiking trails with cliff ladders (designated "Ladder" in Section 3).

- Bicycles and horses are prohibited on hiking trails.

Finally, the AMC gratefully acknowledges the assistance of many groups and individuals in the production of this guide. Special thanks go to Chris Elfring, the former park naturalist who wrote the history, nature, and "Exploring Mount Desert Island" sections of this guide, and to illustrator D.D. Tyler , photographers Tammis Coffin, Earl Brechlin, and Lou Lainey, and cartographer Patrick Dunlavey. Thad Gemski of the AMC Trails Department directed the revision and expansion of the trails section, reviewing worklogs compiled by Peter Williams, editing earlier trail descriptions and writing new ones, and walking the trails with the assistance of Sam Hodder, Bill Deleo, Mark Anderson, Randy Norting, and Ted Detmar. Deborah Wade, Donald Beal, and Kent Mattingly of the National Park Service, and Tammis Coffin of the Friends of Acadia provided critical assistance in reviewing the manuscript.

The AMC earnestly requests your help in keeping this guidebook up to date. When you hike a trail, please check the description in this book. If you find errors in the text or map, or you can suggest improvements, please write the AMC at *Editor, AMC Acadia National Park Guide, Appalachian Mountain Club, 5 Joy Street, Boston MA 02108.*

Abbreviations

The following abbreviations are used in the trail descriptions in Section 3.

min.	minute(s)
hr.	hour(s)
mph	miles per hour
in.	inch(es)
ft.	foot, feet
yd.	yard(s)
mi.	mile(s)
m.	meter(s)
km.	kilometer(s)
est.	estimate
AMC	Appalachian Mountain Club
FR	Forest Route
ME	Maine
NPS	National Park Service
US	United States
USGS	United States Geological Survey

Section One History

by Chris Elfring

WEBSTER defines an island as any piece of land smaller than a continent that is surrounded by the sea. But somehow that doesn't say enough. It doesn't account for the special feel an island has, the special character. An island, even one like Mount Desert that is separated from the mainland by only a few hundred yards of water at hightide, feels separate, isolated, and somehow romantic. Where mountains meet the sea, the landscape is diverse and intriguing. There is the quiet solitude of the deep woods and the rumbling roar of surf crashing on the rocky coast. Breezes carry hints of many environments—the salt air of the sea; the crisp, tingling air of a mountain top in fall; the damp, heavy air near a beaver pond in summer.

Mount Desert Island, home to Acadia National Park, is a crossroads where contrasts are juxtaposed. It is a meeting place of land and ocean, mountain and valley, forest and meadow, fresh water and salt that provides habitat for a wide array of plant and animal life. Here, a landscape of glacially scoured mountains and boulder-tossed coasts tells of the ever-present forces of change in nature. The island tells a tale of human history, too, with its small villages and carriage roads as clues to a vibrant past.

Geologic History

All the earth is a dynamic environment, and MDI is no exception. Just look around and you'll find evidence of change everywhere in the landscape. The scale can be small and swift—such as when a large, old tree falls during a storm—or slow and substantial, such as the erosion of the island's granite cliffs by persistent waves.

Like everywhere on Earth, the geologic history of MDI is defined by the movements of the continental plates, the formation and erosion of mountain chains, the birth and death of seas, and other physical processes. The story begins some 500 million years ago, when the spot where MDI now sits was part of a vast sea. Ancient streams on nearby lands eroded highlands and the sediments washed into the sea, to be compacted into layers of rock over time. These sediments built up at a rate of about an inch every hundred years until they grew to depths of thousands of feet.

Three great periods of deposition and sedimentation are evident on MDI. The oldest remaining rock formation is the Ellsworth Schist, rocks that consist of thinly layered sediments of sand, silt, and mud deposited some 450 to 500 million years ago and then substantially altered—metamorphosed—by heat and pressure; these gray metamorphic rocks are characterized by thin, light-colored, wavy lines. Next oldest is the Bar Harbor series, rocks formed when layers of gravel, coarse and fine sand, and silt were deposited about 400 to 420 million years ago;

these sedimentary rocks are predominantly brown, gray, or green siltstone that splits along its bedding planes. The youngest is the Cranberry Island series, formed from the deposition of massive amounts of volcanic ash and rock fragments, most likely deposited some 380 to 400 million years ago (although there is still some argument over the ages of the Bar Harbor and Cranberry Island series). These rocks show a fine-grained, whitish matrix with embedded rock fragments, with only mild metamorphism.

Next was an event critical in the island's evolution: Approximately 350 to 400 million years ago, miles beneath the earth's surface, a great pool of molten rock began to intrude upward, squeezing up into fractures and other openings and ultimately cooling part way to the surface like a giant bubble. This cooled rock is the coarse, pink granite that forms the core of what is now MDI. You'll see it everywhere; it's the basic rock you walk on as you climb the mountains or boulder-hop along the coast. The MDI granite is composed of quartz (milky gray and glassy), feldspar (usually pink or whitish), and flecks of black hornblende. This period of volcanic intrusion, which ended some 350 million years ago, coincided with major mountain-building processes along the entire East Coast of North America as this continent collided with Europe and Africa. It took eons of erosion for the huge thicknesses of overlying rock to weather away and expose the once-buried pink granite. By about 135 million years ago, the Mount Desert Range showed as a roughly east-west continuous ridge, split here and there by deep stream valleys.

The landscape was to see another major force for change before it would look familiar to today's visitor—

continental glaciation. About a million years ago, the Pleis-
tocene glaciation began. Evidence suggests that at least 9
continental glaciers advanced and retreated over the northern reaches of the globe during the last million years, following a fairly regular pattern: glacial cycles tend to last for
about 100,000 years, with about 80,000 years in glacial
periods and interglacial epochs that last 15,000 to 20,000
years. It was a mere 18,000 years ago when the last of those
nine glaciers spread south out of Canada, a time we call the
Wisconsin glaciation. The southernmost terminus of this
glacier was at Long Island, NY, and the ice sheet covered
most of New England. At its maximum extent, the ice covering MDI was probably a mile thick—four times the
height of Cadillac Mountain. The burden of the weight was
so great that the land compressed. As the ice crept over the
island, it dramatically altered the landscape.

The massive sheets of glacial ice that covered the
island and all of Maine 18,000 years ago moved like rivers
in slow motion, overwhelming anything—whether tree or
rock or mountain—that stood in the way. The glacial ice
and debris polished the granite, sometimes leaving long
striations and other markings. As it moved, the ice carved
the island's mountains into their characteristic rounded
shapes and scoured gentle U-shaped valleys such as the
ones seen from the Tarn or between Cadillac and Pemetic
mountains in the eastern part of MDI. Some of the deep-
ened valleys filled with water, forming deep lakes such as
Echo Lake and Eagle Lake. Somes Sound—with its steep
cliffs, deep water, and shallow mouth—is the only fjord on
the east coast of the United States, a glacially carved valley
that was drowned by the sea. As the glacier melted and
retreated, it left giant boulders, called glacial erratics, scat-

tered across the land (for example, Bubble Rock balanced on the side of South Bubble Mountain). Look at a map of the island: Note the shape of the lakes and the north-south orientation of the mountains, and you will see the path of the glaciers.

When the glaciers withdrew, sea level rose, flooding 300 miles of continental shelf before stopping at the present coastline. Since the ice had stripped the landscape bare of all remnants of past ecosystems, what you see today is fresh by geologic standards—today's landscape, both the physical outline and the current composition of species, began to take shape when the glacier retreated just 13,000 years ago and was established as you see it today only 8,000 years ago.

Since the glacier retreated, wind, water, and weather have continued as forces of change. The relentless lashing of waves continues to shape the coast, the freezing and thawing of water in crevices breaks the granite on its way toward soil, and many other processes cause slow but inevitable alterations in the landscape.

But the most dramatic force of change in recent history is fire. In 1947, MDI saw a fire of awesome destructive power, and it changed the face of the island like no other event in recent times. The stage was set by the weather— 1947 was an extraordinarily dry year, with little if any rain from May through September. October, as is often the case, was a glorious month, the beautiful fall colors seeming especially brilliant against the cloudless blue sky. On Thursday, October 23, 1947, the tinder-dry conditions exploded into fire. How the fire started is still a matter of conjecture: it started inland from Salsbury Cove, in the vicinity of a garbage dump that's no longer there. Perhaps the sun was magnified through a bit of glass, perhaps a careless human act was to blame.

At first, the fire burned slowly, consuming only 169 acres in the first 3 days. But then strong winds fanned the flames and they blasted out of control across the island. At one point, the wind shifted and increased to gale proportions, sending the inferno directly toward Bar Harbor. In less than 3 hours the wildfire traveled 6 miles, leaving a 3-mile wide path of destruction and consuming many of the glorious summer cottages that were along Route 3. The fire raged for 2 weeks, despite valiant efforts of hundreds of volunteer firefighters. When the "all out" signal was finally sounded on November 7, a total of 18,000 acres on the east side of the island had burned, including some 10,000 acres in Acadia National Park. In and around Bar Harbor, at least 5 hotels, 67 summer cottages, 170 homes, and the famous Jackson Laboratory burned. Total damage was estimated at $23 million.

Evidence of the fire's devastation of the community has faded from view, but the fire changed the landscape in many lasting ways. Although destructive, in another sense fire gives a rebirth to the land, consuming dead wood and debris and opening dense forests to new growth. The spruce-fir forest that had monopolized the island was cleared in places so there was space for such sun-loving deciduous trees as the aspen that add lovely golden color to the hillsides in fall. Certain animal populations thrive today on MDI as a result of the fire. For instance, the changes in forest type caused by the fire brought more food for white-tailed deer and beaver, so their populations increased.

Human History

The earliest human use of Mount Desert Island is difficult to trace because the Maine climate is cool and moist, and thus decay robs us of the artifacts that help us decipher pre-recorded history. Deep piles of shells indicate that the island was home to an indigenous people, now called the Abenaki, who lived off the bounty of both sea and land at least 6,000 years ago. Whether the Indians inhabited the island year-round, or whether they were summer or winter visitors is a matter of some debate. You can learn more about them and their culture by visiting the Abbe Museum, a small collection of artifacts located near Sieur de Monts Springs.

We know more about the island's recent human story—its history since the arrival of European explorers. The first was the famous French explorer Samuel de Champlain, who sailed into these waters in 1604. It was Champlain who named the island l'Isle des Monts-déserts, or "island of barren mountains," because its bald peaks are so distinctive when viewed from the sea. Although his exploration was fleeting, it destined this land to be known as part of New France before it became New England.

In 1613, a group of French Jesuits established the first French mission in America on what is now Fernald Point, near the entrance to Somes Sound. But French dominance was not to be. Just as the Jesuits began to build a fort, plant corn, and share their religion with the native people, an English ship commanded by Captain Samuel Argall appeared and destroyed the mission. The island became a no man's land, with the French entrenched to the north and the British to the south. For the next 150 years, settlers avoided this contested territory. The island was best known as a landmark for passing ships.

There is one historical note of interest during this period, however. In 1688, an ambitious young Frenchman immigrated to New France and was granted title to 100,000 acres of land along the Maine coast, including all of MDI. Sieur Antonine de la Mothe Cadillac, a title the young gentleman invented for himself, resided on the island briefly, but failed to establish a feudal estate as he had hoped. He and his bride moved west, where he ultimately gained fame as the founder of Detroit. Cadillac Mountain, which bears his name, was originally called Green Mountain but was renamed by the park's first superintendent in an effort to highlight the island's history.

The island, its claim continually disputed, was used as a hiding place for French frigates during the French and Indian wars between 1613 and 1740. When the French were defeated in 1759, the British claimed New England as its own and the coast and island were opened to English, and later American, settlers. This brought the first pioneers, a hardy folk who generally drew their livings from the sea. Often, they settled first on the outer islands— Baker Island, the Cranberry Isles—because these were most convenient to the fishing areas and shipping lanes. Abraham Somes and James Richardson brought their families to MDI in 1760, establishing the first permanent settlement at what is now Somesville. By 1820, the island was thriving—farming and lumbering had joined fishing and shipbuilding as major occupations. Canneries, lobster pounds, and boatyards were mainstays of the local economy. People's lives were tied to the sea; it was the major source of food, the primary employer, and the only real transportation route for people or goods.

The island's fate took a curious and critical turn in the mid-1800s. This was when the island was "discovered" by painter Thomas Cole, founder of the Hudson River School of painting. He filled his sketchbook with enticing drawings and returned to New York; lured by these images of rugged beauty, others soon followed. These first visitors were called "rusticators," for they enjoyed a relatively rustic lifestyle, renting rooms from farmers and eating simple fare. Soon, though, the fresh salt air, beautiful scenery, and relaxed pace drew so many guests that local accommodations were overflowing. In 1868, steamboat service began between Boston and MDI, and the first of what was to be an explosion of hotels—the Island House—was built near the first steamboat wharf in Southwest Harbor. In 1872, the national magazine *Harper's* featured Eden (renamed Bar Harbor in 1919) as *the* place to vacation. By 1880 the island hosted 30 hotels, some simple, but some grand, like the Rodick House, which could house 600 guests. From 1868–1882 (often referred to as the Hotel Era) at least one hotel was built or significantly expanded each year. Tourism had come of age as a major industry on MDI.

By the 1890s, the town was the undisputed king of vacation resorts. The island became a summer retreat for America's wealthiest and most influential families as the Rockefellers, Morgans, Fords, Vanderbilts, Carnegies, and Astors chose to spend their summers here. Tiring of hotel life, these visitors transformed the landscape into a haven of elegant mansions and estates, euphemistically called cottages. In a booming economy, these grew to include 40,

50, and even 60 rooms. One 80-room cottage had 28 complete bathrooms. The average cottage employed at least 10 servants. Route 3 between Salsbury Cove and Bar Harbor was known as Millionaire's Row. The Gay Nineties social scene was thriving: teas, lawn parties, extravagant picnics, horse races, even that new game, golf, occupied the long leisure hours of the privileged class.

The seemingly endless growth and development worried some of the wealthy summer visitors. George Dorr of Boston, together with Charles Eliot, president of Harvard University, sought to preserve the island's natural character and in 1901 purchased portions of the island for a park. Joined by John D. Rockefeller, Jr., and other residents, they patched together a quilt of mountains and valleys and coast, and in July 1916 it was declared Sieur de Monts National Monument. When it was renamed Lafayette National Park in 1919, it became the first national park east of the Mississippi. In 1929, the park was renamed Acadia National Park and the only mainland part of the park, Schoodic Peninsula, was added. Portions of Isle au Haut, a remote island reached by boat from Stonington, were added to the park in 1943.

John D. Rockefeller, Jr., proved to be an especially important advocate for the park. In all, Rockefeller generously donated nearly 1/3 of the park's acreage. He was also responsible for Acadia's carriage roads: Soon after residents at last won their battle in 1913 to allow automobiles on the island, Rockefeller decided to design and finance a network of roads exclusively for carriages. His goal was to provide the maximum enjoyment of the scenery with the least disruption of the environment. Built between 1917 and 1933, the 57-mile network winds throughout the eastern side of the island and still provides visitors with a quiet retreat where they can enjoy panoramic ocean vistas, hemlock-covered mountainsides, small waterfalls, and other sights at a leisurely pace. The two main entrances to the system at Jordan Pond and Lower Hadlock Pond are marked by gatehouses—English Tudor Revival–style homes of cut stone, red brick, and steep, tiled roofs where the gatekeepers lived. Special care was taken to build the 16 bridges scattered through the system. Each of the hand-carved granite structures is unique—Hemlock Bridge, completed in 1924, for instance, is a massive Gothic-arched structure spanning 185 feet across Maple Spring Brook. Bubble Pond Bridge, completed in 1928, is an elliptical-arched structure with rustic details.

Even as the park grew and took shape, forces for change were converging that would again alter MDI's landscape. For more than 40 years, the wealthy had dominated the island's life, but the Great Depression, the imposition of personal income taxes, the burgeoning costs of maintenance, and the rigor of World War II marked the beginning of the end for the extravagant Cottage Era. The final blow was the great fire of 1947, which consumed many of the great estates. The fire also changed the social landscape significantly, for in ravaging the beautiful wooden mansions of the Gay Nineties, it ended an era of wealth and opulence and opened the way for today's style of tourism.

But while the great fire of 1947 changed the character of the island in many ways, MDI still retained its popularity as a summer retreat. The summer population is almost 3 times the 10,000 people who live on the island year-round, and tourism remains the most important industry. Acadia National Park hosts some three million recreational visitors each year, making it one of the most frequently visited parks in the nation.

The island has continued to see changes, though none so dramatic as the 1947 fire. In 1968, the National Park Service built the Hulls Cove Visitor Center off Route 3 to help people better enjoy their time on the island. In 1970, as crowds increased, the Park Loop Road was designated one-way to enhance visitor safety and provide a more pleasant experience. In 1979, the famed Jordan Pond House—a quaint, rustic structure—burned to the ground. It was rebuilt, though, and the new, award-winning building soon gained its own loyal fans—keeping the tradition of stopping for fresh, hot popovers and tea on the lawn alive for a new generation of island visitors.

After more than 20 years of often acrimonious debate, congressional legislation was passed in 1986 that clearly defined the boundaries of Acadia National Park—a compromise that finally allowed park managers to have a long-term vision of what resources to plan for and that assured the local community the park would not grow unchecked.

Recently Acadia's historic carriage roads have also undergone renewal. Until 1960 the roads and their bridges were maintained by John D. Rockefeller. After his death the roads fell into disrepair and dwindling use. Then in 1990 a three-phase restoration project began. The first step, completed that year, was the privately funded restoration of a 2-mile section of carriage road and the clearing of several historic vistas. A public-private partnership between the park service and the nonprofit group Friends of Acadia is to complete the restoration and maintenance of the roads. Now included in the National Register of Historic Places, the carriage road system has become a retreat for walkers, bicyclists, cross country skiers, and horses and carriages. Given the renewed uses of this delightful system, park managers ask that you treat these resources with respect and care so future visitors may enjoy them as well.

Recent years have also brought an increased awareness of the many problems faced by our national parks— and Acadia is no stranger to these threats. Air pollution, water-quality degradation, the invasion of exotic species: park managers today must cope with numerous direct and indirect threats to park resources. Pressures from adjacent land uses have increased as well, something visible to anyone driving around the island. During the island's golden era, the population was high but the people congregated in a few relatively confined communities; today, we all dream of our own little place in the woods, the impact of which is far greater. The remaining wild habitats outside the park are increasingly fragmented.

One trend evident on the island today is a refreshing echo of the past: There seems to be a resurgence of the spirit of stewardship that George Dorr, Charles Eliot, and other founders of the park felt. The people who live and visit the island are again actively involved in caring for the park. Volunteers, some working for as little as half a day, are helping maintain park trails, inventory park resources, and assist park staff. The rewards to the park and to the individuals involved are great.

Nature on
Mount Desert Island

by Chris Elfring
illustrations by D.D. Tyler

MOUNT Desert Island (MDI) is small—about 18 miles long and 14 miles wide—but it is a microcosm of the northern coastal landscape. It is rugged, a bit raw, and refreshing. MDI is home to at least 50 species of mammals, 325 species of birds, 1000 species of flowering plants, and many other living things. The following pages describe some of the most common species you may encounter as you explore Mount Desert Island and Acadia National Park.

Plant Life

Part of what has attracted visitors to MDI for so many years is the physical environment, the blend of forests and meadows and marshes. It is the North Woods in miniature, where a visitor can learn to identify the trees, wildflowers, shrubs, and other plants common all along the Maine coast. The island is home to a diverse assortment of plants, from the ghostly gray Indian Pipe that hides in the debris of the damp forest floor to the elegant white pines. In all, there are at least 1000 species of flowering plants on the island.

For many visitors, the island's forests have a special appeal, for here the cool, refreshing smell of the northern coniferous forest overlaps with the colorful beauty of the temperate deciduous forest. There are places on the island reminiscent of the Labrador shore, a pine barren in New Jersey, and a mountain summit in Tennessee. Three general forest types dominate: spruce-fir, northern hardwood, and a mixture of the two. Overall, about 35 percent of the island is coniferous spruce-fir forest, 20 percent deciduous forest, 40 percent mixed forest, and 5 percent open water and rock.

As you hike, note the predominant forest type for a clue to the history of the area. The great fire of 1947 burned 18,000 acres on MDI during 2 weeks of tremendous destruction. But just as the island people rebuilt the town of Bar Harbor, still vigorous but of a different character, nature restored the landscape. Today, young forests of aspen, maple, and other sun-loving plants fill the once-burned sections of the island, while the unburned areas retain the island's older, evergreen forests. Even from the top of Cadillac Mountain, you can determine the fire's impact—the lighter green areas you see are the young forests; the darker green areas are the older, spruce-fir forests.

Common Coniferous Trees

Eastern white pine (*Pinus strobus*) is a tall, elegant, cone-bearing evergreen. Needles are soft, blue-green, 2 to 4 inches long, and grow 5 to a cluster. Cones are long and slender; the bark is dark and deeply furrowed. The overall shape is delicate and soft, as compared to the more robust-looking red pine and the scraggly pitch pine. White pines

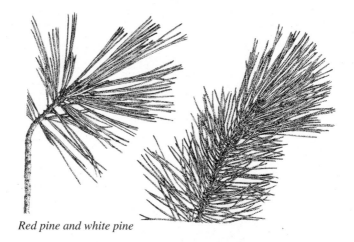

Red pine and white pine

prefer fertile, well-drained soils, while other pines tolerate poorer conditions. White pine was the colonies' chief export to England—the wood is strong, straight, and lightweight, ideal for ship masts and other construction. The King of England reserved all white pines over 2 feet in diameter for the use of the crown, a fact that contributed to the discontent leading to the Revolutionary War. The record white pine in New England was 240 feet tall, but by the early 1900s all the virgin white pines were harvested. Specimens today rarely reach 100 feet.

Red pine (*Pinus resinosa*) is named for the distinctive red hue of the bark and for its pale red wood. It grows tall and straight, and its rich green needles come in bundles of 2, each about 5 or 6 inches long. The reddish bark looks like flat, scaly plates. For a few days in early spring, numerous red clusters of pollen-bearing flowers bloom at the tips of the branches; red pine cones are oval and about 2 inches long. It often grows in gravelly or sandy soil and on rocky ridges.

Pitch pine (*Pinus rigida*) grows where few other trees can withstand the rigors of wind and salt, often on open granite ledges along the coast and on mountain summits. In Acadia, pitch pine grows in dry, rocky sites usually exposed to the south or west. These exposed locations result in gnarled, irregular trees, and in old age the limbs are often misshapen and tufted with scant foliage. The needles grow in bundles of 3 (think "pitch" as in baseball—1-2-3, you're out); are coarse, stiff, and twisted; and vary from 1 1/2 to 5 inches long. The bark of this fire-resistant species is thick, reddish purple, and divided into scaly plates by deep furrows. Cones are stout, about 1 to 3 inches long; each scale is armed with a small thorn on the tip. Cones grow closely attached to the branches or even to the trunk, where they remain for years. The tree is rich in resin—hence the name—and was sometimes called torch pine or candle-wood since torches can be made from the knots where the resin is most concentrated. The resin also makes the wood quite resistant to water decay.

Red spruce (*Picea rubens*) is perhaps the most abundant tree on MDI and a principal timber tree throughout Maine, forming dark, dense stands. Like all spruces, it has short (1/2-inch), stiff needles that grow individually around the twig. To the touch, each needle is 4-sided. Cones are egg shaped, 1 to 1 1/2 inches long, with flaring scales; they fall as soon as they shed their winged seeds. Compared to the white spruce, the red has shorter, almost yellow-green needles and a red-yellow cast to the bark. Its egg-shaped cone

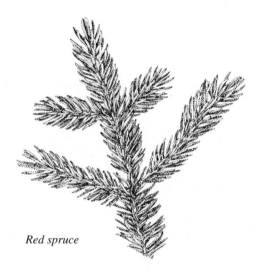

Red spruce

is smaller, and its bark is shaggy rather than smooth. Its growth is more open and the top is typically conical. Red spruce is more common inland.

White spruce (*Picea glauca*) can be identified by smell—crush some needles and notice why it is sometimes called skunk spruce. It is a graceful, symmetrical tree, characterized by bluish green needles about ¹/₃-inch long and long, oval cones. The bark is typically smooth, with a bluish-white cast, and fine hairs on the leaves and twigs create a whitish appearance. White spruce typically has a slender, tapered top, and is more common along the shoreline, such as near Seawall picnic area.

Eastern hemlock (*Tsuga canadensis*) is one of the most beautiful forest trees, with its delicate, silvery foliage and small, perfectly formed cones. The needles are flat and short (1/3 inch), growing in flat rows from the twig. Underneath, you'll find slight white-blue stripes. Cones are small, only about 1/2 inch long, and grow from the end of twigs. This is a shade- and moisture-loving tree, favoring damp, cool stream valleys, such as the carriage road between Bubble Pond and Eagle Lake. The thick bark, which gives the tree good fire resistance, sometimes peels in older trees. The bark is rich in tannin, useful for dyeing and tanning leather, and was once popular as a curative for burns and sores.

Balsam fir (*Abies balsamea*) is common in the island's moist forests, often in the company of spruces. A steeple-shaped tree with graceful branches, the smell of its crushed needles is sure to remind you of Christmas. Its cylindrical cones (2 to 4 inches) grow erect and are sometimes deep purple; its flat needles (1/2 inch) are shiny,

Balsam fir

appearing dark green on top and silvery underneath. Like hemlock, the needles grow along a single plane, giving the boughs a flat appearance. A key to identifying firs— they are flat (the individual needles and the boughs), friendly (stroke a branch and it feels soft), fragrant (the smell of Christmas), and flammable (note the resin blisters on the bark).

Northern white cedar (*Thuja occidentalis*) has characteristic scalelike yellow-green foliage (like tiny, interlocking plates) that completely covers its branches. Crush a sprig for a pleasant, pungent aroma. The bark is brown, distinctly ridged, and peels in stringy, fibrous strands. Its small cones are bell shaped, about 1/2 inch long, and grow in erect clusters near the ends of twigs. The tree grows primarily in cool, damp areas along the coast, lake shores, and streams, and sometimes on damp mountain slopes. The wood is soft and durable and was used for shingles, canoes, and a variety of other purposes. Often called Arbor Vitae, a latinized French name for "tree of life," it's said to have cured the men of Jacques Cartier's Canadian expedition of a disease, probably scurvy. They brought the tree back to Paris, making it the first American tree cultivated in Europe.

Common Deciduous Trees

Bigtooth aspen (*Populus grandidentata*), often called poplar, grows 30 to 40 feet tall, with trunks at times reaching 2 feet in diameter. The bark is smooth and yellow-green or gray. The leaves are heart shaped with large marginal teeth. It has downy leaf buds and round leaf stems. Overall, this species is larger than quaking aspen, which is smaller and has finer marginal teeth on its leaves. The 2 species often grow together, although the overall range of bigtooth aspen is smaller. The tree is most conspicuous in early spring, when it is one of the first trees to bloom. Long tassels of greenish-gray blossoms appear even before the leaves are fully developed. As the seeds release from the tree, they float through the air like a mistimed snowstorm. In autumn, the leaves turn brilliant yellow-gold.

Quaking aspen (*Populus tremuloides*) is a small to medium-sized tree known for the distinctive way its leaves rustle in the slightest breeze. Its heart-shaped leaves are smaller than bigtooth aspen, with fine teeth along the margins. The leaf stems are flattened at right angles to the blade of the leaf, a structural oddity that makes them tremble in any wind. The bark is smooth and chalk white to yellow-green or gray, generally lighter than the bigtooth aspen, and can be mistaken for gray birch. Its buds

Quaking aspen

are shiny. Quaking aspen usually grows to 20 to 40 feet in height, sometimes in groves but often mixed with other species, with trunks up to 1 foot in diameter. It often grows in burned-over areas or recently cleared land—making it a good indicator of areas burned in MDI's devastating fire of 1947. This abundant tree turns bright yellow in the fall. Beavers rely on aspen for food and dam-building materials.

American beech (*Fagus grandifolia*) is common on MDI. Look for a large, handsome tree with pale gray bark, either smooth or mottled with dark blotches. The foliage has distinct marginal teeth and parallel straight veins. In spring, it is bright green; by summer it is darker and stiff, the quality of newly minted paper money. In autumn the leaves turn yellow and rust, and, unlike most deciduous trees, beech leaves often cling to the tree long into winter. After the first hard frost, the trees drop a crop of beechnuts—small, sweet, triangular nuts that are rich in oil. They were gathered for food in colonial days, and used to fatten hogs for market. Beech trees prefer good, moist soil, and settlers often used them as indicators of good farmland. Beechnuts were an important food for the passenger pigeon, and the cutting of beech to open agricultural land may have contributed to that bird's extinction.

White birch (*Betula papyrifera*), also called paper birch, has a brilliant white trunk and fine, papery bark. The white bark is smooth, showing narrow horizontal slits and sometimes dark, triangular branch scars. Birch leaves are 2 to 4 inches long, rounded at the base and tapering to a point, with a fine, double-toothed margin; they are sometimes confused with quaking aspen. In autumn, the leaves turn

White birch

brilliant yellow. Today, birch are rarely more than 60 feet tall, but they grew twice as high in virgin forests. Birch grow on mountainsides and in meadows and lowlands, and are one of the first species to move into disturbed areas. The species reproduces both by seed and sprouts. Birch bark is rich in oil and thus both waterproof and resistant to rot—so resistant, in fact, that you'll often find limbs on the forest floor where the wood has crumbled but the bark remains intact. White birch were used by Native Americans to build canoes and cover tepees.

Yellow birch (*Betula lutea*) is a very large tree, sometimes still found growing to over 100 feet high. The bark is silvery bronze and peels in irregular, thin, papery curls. This species favors moist woods and shaded ravines. The leaves are similar to white birch, and also turn bright yellow in fall. In spring the male catkins are more than 3 inches long while the female are less than 1 inch. Indians collected the rotted inner wood within downed bark, dried it, and carried it with them as tinder to start fires. Small twigs of yellow birch are said to have been used as toothpicks by Indians and settlers; they taste refreshingly of mint.

Red maple (*Acer rubrum*) earns its name throughout the year. In late April and early May, small clusters of red flowers emerge, and when the young leaves unfold they also are reddish. Red veins and stems keep their color all summer. Then in autumn, it is one of the first trees to show its fall color—blazing crimson or maroon-red, of course. This is a medium-sized (20 to 40 feet tall), lowlands tree, often found in moist, rich soils near marshes and along lake shores and streams. Red maple is a symmetrical tree with dark gray bark; the smooth bark of younger trees may form plates with age. Leaves (3 to 5 inches) have 3 main

Red maple

triangular lobes with numerous sharp, V-shaped notches, as compared to the softer U-shaped notches of the sugar maple. Most commercial maple syrup is made from sugar maple, but the sap of red maple also can be boiled down to produce syrup.

Sugar maple (*Acer saccharum*) is the largest of the maples found on MDI, sometimes growing 40 to 60 feet high, with diameters of 1 to 2 feet. Leaves are 3 to 6 inches with 5 triangular lobes and numerous wavy U-shaped notches (as compared to the sharp, V-shaped notches of the red maple). In fall, the leaves turn brilliant shades of yellow, orange, and red. The gray bark forms plates that become flaky with age. Seeds are paired, winged fruits (called helicopters by many youths) that are important food sources for birds, squirrels, and other small animals. As the name implies, this is the species of maple-syrup fame. Sugaring begins in March when the sap first begins to flow; 40 gallons of sap will boil down to about 1 gallon of syrup.

Striped maple (*Acer pensylvanicum*), also called moosewood, goosefoot maple, and even campers' TP, is a distinctive, small, under-story tree. It typically grows 5 to 15 feet tall, and seldom exceeds 25 feet. Its leaves are quite large (5 to 6 inches), however, with 3 lobes, and are reminiscent of a goose's foot. They can be useful to campers caught without proper bathroom facilities. Most noticeable, though, is the pale green bark and the long, white, vertical stripes that run down the trunk of young trees, particularly visible in winter. In fall, the leaves turn a pale yellow that seems to glow in the deep forest light. Although moose are uncommon on MDI, in other areas moose browse on the sweet young shoots of this species.

Northern red oak (*Quercus rubra*) has reddish-brown bark with distinct reddish furrows. Its leaves grow 5 to 8 inches long, deeply cut into 7 to 11 angular, pointed lobes. Red-oak acorns are large, sometimes looking out of proportion to their caps, and they cling to the tree in winter. It is a stately tree, with a thick trunk and broadly rounded crown. In spring, the young leaves unfurl a tinted pink; in fall, after the peak of the color season, they turn a deep wine red.

Scrub oak (*Quercus ilicifolia*), also called bear oak, is one of the island's rarest native trees. Here, it is growing at the extreme northeastern end of its range—it is more typical of the hot, sandy plains of New Jersey. On MDI, it grows

Scrub oak

mostly as a shrub on dry ledges on the southwest and south faces of Acadia Mountain, diminishing as you climb down, and in a few other spots on St. Sauveur Mountain. Its leaves are small (2 to 5 inches), with shallow notches and fewer lobes than red oak.

Common Wildflowers

Wildflowers are plentiful on the island, beginning in the early spring when the mayflower, or trailing arbutus, blossoms. The spring display of rhodora is particularly beautiful. The procession of flowers continues until autumn, when the witch hazel blooms. You'll find the most showy flowers along the roadsides and in open terrain; in the forest, you'll need a keener eye. As you're hiking the coastal trails or open meadows, you'll see that there is a touch of truth to the children's tale of Miss Rumphius, who in her quest to leave the earth more beautiful than she found it, scatters lupine seeds all along the coast of Maine. Although not a native species, the violet and pink spires of this flower dress roadsides and other disturbed soils all across the island.

Canada dogwood

IN THE FOREST

Canada dogwood (*Cornus canadensis*), also called bunchberry, is common in the woods of MDI. It grows close to the ground (6 to 8 inches high), often in extensive patches. Leaves occur in a whorl of 6, with parallel leaf veins as in most other dogwoods. In May and June, 4 rounded white bracts (they look like petals) surround a central cluster of very small, greenish flowers, giving the appearance of a single showy blossom. Later, tightly clustered scarlet berries form.

Canada mayflower (*Maianthemum canadense*), or wild lily of the valley, grows in cool, damp woods and semi-shaded clearings. It grows 3 to 6 inches high, an erect stem with 2 (sometimes 3) leaves with heart-shaped leaf bases and prominent parallel veins. The small, cream-colored flowers (out in May and June) have four petals and grow in a terminal spike; the stamens give the flower a fuzzy look. When berries form, they are white with spots, later turning pale and then bright red.

Indian pipe

Indian pipe (*Monotropa uniflora*) is a strangely surreal plant, a transluscent white stalk (4 to 10 inches high) with a single white, sometimes almost pale pink, flower nodding from the tip. The plant has no chlorophyll, thus the ghostly color; it is a saprophytic and parasitic plant that feeds on decaying organic matter and sometimes the roots of other plants. It grows from June to September in dark, damp forests, and is often almost hidden among the litter of the forest floor.

Painted trillium (*Trillium undulatum*) is a rare but extraordinarily beautiful lily found in damp woodlands and shaded stream valleys. It grows 8 to 20 inches high, an erect stem with 3 broad, oval leaves that taper to a point. From this whorl, a single flower blooms in late May or early June—3 delicate, wavy-edged, white petals, each streaked with a crimson blaze at the base.

Solomon's seal (*Polygonatum biflorum*) and **False Solomon's seal** (*Smilacina racemosa*) are also woodland lilies. They appear similar, each having oval, pointed leaves about 2 to 6 inches long that alternate along a gracefully reclining stem. True Solomon's seal has its flowers in the leaf axils; they are yellowish, $2/3$ inch long, and hang in 5 to 10 pairs from under the stem. False Solomon's seal has tiny, cream-colored flowers borne in terminal clusters. Both species bloom in June.

Starflower (*Trientalis borealis*) favors cool evergreen forests. A member of the primrose family, the plant is an erect stem 4 to 6 inches high topped with a whorl of 5 to 9 shiny, narrow leaves (each 2 to 3 inches long). In late May and June, 1 or 2 fragile white flowers bloom, each a star with 6 to 7 points.

Trailing Arbutus (*Epigaea repens*) is one of the first wildflowers to blossom on MDI each spring. This low, creeping plant blooms as early as mid-April, showing dense little clusters of pink and white 5-petaled flowers. The leaves are oval, leathery, and evergreen, and there is a trailing, hairy stem. Trailing arbutus often grows in dense mats in semishaded coniferous or mixed woodlands.

Wintergreen (*Gaultheria procumbens*), or checkerberry, is a small, creeping plant you might see along the edge of a semishaded trail. The evergreen leaves are thick, shiny, and oval, perhaps only 1 to 2 inches long. In late June and early July, 2 small, bell-shaped flowers droop from under the leaves, often quite hidden. Later, the small berries are bright red. When crushed, both the fruit and the leaves give a fragrant, wintergreen aroma.

IN OPEN TERRAIN

Beach pea (*Lathyrus japonicus*) is a low (1 to 2 feet high) plant with showy purple-to-pink pealike flowers. Leaves have 8 to 12 oval leaflets; at the tip is a tendril used for climbing. Beach pea grows prolifically along the upper shoreline of sandy and rocky beaches—you'll find it, for instance, all along the shores of Baker Island. It blooms June to August.

Bluet (*Houstonia caerulea*) is a tiny, pale blue or whitish flower with a yellow eye. Each solitary flower has 4 small petals and grows atop an erect 3-to-6-inch stem; leaves along the stem are paired, short, and narrow. Bluet blooms, sometimes in large colonies, in May and June.

Fireweed (*Epilobium angustifolium*), as the name implies, often grows in old burns and along roadsides. A member of the evening primrose family, it grows in clumps of plants 3 to 7 feet tall. The pink flowers have 4 rounded petals growing on slender spikes; flowering begins at the bottom of the spike and moves upward. Leaves are alternate, 3 to 8 inches long, and slender. It blooms in July and August.

Harebell (*Campanula rotundifolia*) is a delicate plant that grows 6 to 18 inches tall, often tucked among boulders along the coast or in grassy areas at high elevations. The flowers are small purple-blue bells. It blooms from mid-July to September.

Orange hawkweed (*Hieracium aurantiacum*) is a showy, roadside flower—a small, bright orange, many-petaled flower atop a 1-to-2-foot hairy stem. Its blooms appear from June to September.

Ox-eye daisy (*Chrysanthemum leucanthemum*) is a common, large, white daisy. The flowers are about 2 inches across, with a yellow disk depressed in the center. It grows 1 to 3 feet tall and blooms from June to August.

Queen Anne's lace (*Daucus carota*), more correctly called wild carrot, is a lovely wildflower with extremely flat, lacelike clusters of white flowers and finely divided, feathery leaves. Wild carrot blooms from May to October.

Wild lupine (*Lupinus perennis*) is a striking plant in the pea family, with spikes of small, multiple, pealike flowers in violet-blue and pink. The leaves are palmate, radiating into 7 to 9 segments, and the plant grows 1 to 2 feet tall. It prefers dry soils, often growing in meadows and along roadsides. Introduced from the Pacific Northwest, it blooms in June and July.

Yarrow (*Achillea millefolium*) grows 1 to 2 feet tall, capped with a flat cluster of tiny, white flowers, each with five petals. The alternate leaves are soft, feathery, almost fernlike, and wonderfully aromatic when crushed. Yarrow originally came from Europe and blooms from June to August.

Common Shrubs
Lowbush blueberry, whether the early variety (*Vaccinium vacillans*) or the late (*Vaccinium angustifolium*), are an unforgettable treat for summer visitors. These low shrubs generally grow 1 to 2 feet tall; the leaves are small,

oval, and sometimes fine-
ly serrated, dull green
above and whitish under-
neath. The berries are
dark blue with a
dusting of white
powder and are quite
edible, of course.
Look for blueberries from
late June to September in
dry, sunny meadows, espe-
cially along roads, trails, and
carriage roads. **Black
huckleberry** (*Gaylus-
sacia baccata*) looks
similar, but its leaves
are speckled on both
surfaces with yellowish resin
dots and the berries are less tasty.

Lowbush blueberry

Mountain cranberry (*Vaccinium vitis-idaea*) is a creeping, mat-forming plant with small, egg-shaped, odorless
evergreen leaves. The underside of the leathery leaves is
dotted with tiny black spots (which you may need a hand
lens to see). Bell-shaped pink or red flowers bloom in June
and July; red fruits ripen in late summer. **Small** and **large
cranberry** (*Vaccinium oxycoccus* and *V. macrocarpon*)
are closely related species found in bogs.

Sheep laurel (*Kalmia angustifolia*), also called lambkill
because the foliage may be poisonous to livestock, is a
small shrub (up to 3 feet high) with leathery, evergreen
leaves. The leaves are oblong to narrow, 1 to 2 inches

long, and sometimes rust colored underneath when young. The flowers are delicate, 5-sided cups of deep pink that grow in clusters high on the plant. Sheep laurel is common in bogs and tucked into crevices on exposed mountain ridges, and it blooms mid-June to mid-July.

Rhodora (*Rhododendron canadense*) is a wild azalea that favors poor soils and acid bogs, and gives a spectacular show of spring color in Acadia. Its purplish flowers appear before its leaves, typically in late May or early June. Individual flowers are slender and more delicate than many azaleas. The plant grows 2 to 3 feet tall; the bright green leaves are blunt tipped and somewhat hairy. Look for it in damp areas such as swamp and pond edges.

Rugosa rose (*Rosa rugosa*), often called seaside rose, is a wild rose that grows in dense thickets along the shores of many coastal islands—MDI, Baker, and the Cranberry Isles all have showy patches. The stems are thickly covered with sharp bristles and the leaves are deeply wrinkled. Mid-June through August brings fragrant, 5-petaled flowers, either deep purple-pink or white and 3 to 4 inches across. Later in summer, shiny orange fruits—rose hips—provide more color as well as food for wildlife.

Staghorn sumac (*Rhus typhina*) grows either as a shrub or a small tree, with a straggling, forked appearance and distinctive erect fruit clusters that resemble a deer's antlers "in velvet." The leaves are large, made up of 11 to 31 toothed leaflets. The bark is dark and smooth; twigs are hairy.

Sweet fern (*Comptonia peregrina*) is a low bush with woody stem and branches, but with fernlike foliage that smells wonderfully sweet when crushed. The leaves are slender, 3 to 6 inches long, and lobed on all margins. It is common along roads, trails, and other hot, sunny places.

Dwarf juniper (*Juniperus communis*) is a low-growing evergreen shrub, often found in mats along the coast. The scale-like foliage is stiff, 3-sided, whitish green, and grows in whorls of 3. It has small, dark blue berries that appear dusted with white powder. The plant is food for grouse, deer, and small birds and mammals. Look for it along the Shore Path near Otter Point or on the Ship Harbor Trail.

Ferns, Mosses, and Lichens

Bracken fern (*Pteridium aquilinium*) is probably the island's most common fern. The fronds are broad, coarse, and spread horizontally in 3 parts. Spores form in narrow lines close to the margin of the leaflets. Its fiddleheads, the new uncoiled fronds, are edible. The full-grown fronds develop a toxin that sometimes poisons grazing animals. Bracken ferns have fire-resistant roots and thus are quick to reinvade after a fire. They are commonly found in sunny meadows and along roadsides, or in drier woods.

Christmas fern (*Polystichum arostichoides*) takes its name from the shape of the leaflets on its fronds—each is shaped like a tiny Christmas stocking. The leathery, dark green leaves grow 2 to 3 feet tall. It has erect, spore-bearing fronds surrounded by shorter, sterile ones. Withered spore cases turn cinnamon brown. This fern is often found among rocks, on rocky ledges, or in rocky parts of the woods.

Cinnamon fern (*Osmunda cinnamonea*) is a large, grace-ful fern that grows in circular clumps. In late spring slen-der, spore-bearing fronds grow in the center of the crown—first green, then maturing to a rich cinnamon color. These stalks wither by midsummer. The leaflets and tips are more pointed than those on the similar interrupted fern. It grows best in damp, shady places.

Interrupted fern (*Osmunda claytoniana*) grows to be 2 to 4 feet tall. It takes it name from its growth habit—it has a few brown fertile fronds that "interrupt" the sterile green ones. Fertile fronds are erect; look for 4 or more pairs of small, dense, spore-bearing leaflets midway up the frond. While it resembles the cinnamon fern, its fronds have a dull surface and its leaflets are more rounded.

Hair cap moss (*Polytrichum commune*) grows in dense, dark green mats, often along the edges of trails and other sunny spots. Very soft to the touch, its stem is ringed with soft, narrow, pointed leaves. When wet, the leaves stand at right angles to the stem, but when dry they fold against the stem to conserve moisture. Spore cases grow on small (2 to 4 inches) stalks, each covered by a tiny cap that is easily transported by the wind.

Sphagnum mosses (*Sphagnum sps.*) typically grow any-where that is wet, often in dense mats. These mosses can absorb many times their weight in water, like living sponges. They can make the ground look deceptively dry, only to lure an unsuspecting hiker toward wet boots. The color varies by species from bright green to yellowish-green to reddish; the only moss with "leafy" branches topped with a characteristic compact rosette.

Hair cap moss

Lichens are composed of two distinct and dissimilar plants—a fungus and an alga, living together in situations where neither could exist alone. The fungus parasitizes the alga for food but provides a moist, protected environment in which the alga thrives. The alga photosynthesizes to produce food for itself and the fungus. Lichens vary greatly in size, shape, color, and habit. Most are ashy gray or greenish, but some are deep green, pink, and sulfur yellow. Lichens are often described as *crustose* (forming crusts on trees and rocks), *foliose* (leaflike, or having thin, broad, papery structures), or *fruiticose* (branching, including both upright growers and ones that hang in threadlike streamers). Distinguishing lichens can be difficult, as some fungi resemble lichens so closely that you would need a microscope to really see the difference. If it's attached to rock with no other organic matter present, it is definitely a lichen. Some common lichens follow:

Common reindeer moss (*Cladonia rangiferina*) is a lichen, not a moss. It grows as an ashy gray, intricately branched mass, which to an active imagination looks like tiny reindeer antlers. It is actually so named, however, because it is a major food source for reindeer in the Arctic.

British soldiers (*Cladonia cristatella*) is a fruticose lichen, growing as tiny, coral-like stalks with bright red caps. Look for it in sunny spots, growing on decaying logs or old stumps.

Boulder lichen grows as a yellow-green, flat crust on rocks everywhere on MDI. Growing slowly over hundreds of years, it forms "fairy rings" on the rock. It plays a role in slowly breaking rock down into soil.

Map lichen is another common crustose lichen, typically bright green or yellow green and appearing in maplike designs on rock.

Animal Life

Because of the great diversity of habitats available on this island of contrasts between mountain and sea, MDI is home to a diversity of animal life. About 50 species of mammals and more than 300 species of birds are found in the park—some as permanent residents, others as migratory visitors. There are also many amphibians and reptiles, including 5 kinds of snakes (none are poisonous).

Most visitors looking for wildlife hope to see mammals—there is something especially appealing about these warm-blooded, fur-bearing relatives. MDI is home to mammals ranging from tiny shrews that are rarely seen to fairly common white-tailed deer. Your best chance of seeing any wildlife comes with understanding: Know where the animals are most likely to be seen and what time of day they are active; then be patient and observant. The reality, however, is that mammals are among the most elusive of island life, and many are nocturnal, so at best we see squirrels and chipmunks and perhaps an occasional glimpse of some other shy creature. Still, there are other ways to "see" wildlife. Look for clues—a chewed stump that indicates the presence of beaver, deer tracks in damp soil, scat. And then look again for the more subtle clues hidden in the landscape—silver hairs on a hollow log that show where a raccoon bedded down; a distinct browse line in cedar foliage created by deer eating to the upper limit of their reach; a tiny pile of discarded bracts (a midden) left atop a boulder where a squirrel sat to eat the seeds from a pine cone.

Mammals

Little brown bat (*Myotis lucifugus*), or little brown myotis, is suitably named—it weighs $1/4$ to $1/3$ ounce and has a wingspan of less than 3 inches. It leaves its daytime retreats—hollow trees, buildings, caves—at dusk to feed on flying insects and returns to the roosting sites just before dawn. Its flight is erratic as it pursues its prey.

Beaver (*Castor canadensis*) watching should be part of every visitor's experience on MDI. An hour or two before dusk, station yourself at one of the island's many beaver ponds and wait. With luck, you'll see this nocturnal animal busy about its tasks, perhaps dragging sticks as food or building materials for its dam or lodge. You might hear the sharp slap of its tail against the water—a warning to other beavers. You're less likely to see beaver on land as water is their favored habitat, although they come ashore to gather food (aspen is a favorite) and make repairs to the dam. Look for a small, brown, furry head, almost doglike, moving swiftly enough to leave a gentle V-shaped wake. Also look for the lodge, a conical mound of sticks and mud; the entrance is underwater for added protection. Contrary to folklore, the scaly, flat tail is not used to haul mud, but it does act as a rudder to help it steer while swimming.

Beaver

Eastern chipmunk (*Tamias striatus*) is a common campground companion. These small, squirrel-like animals have white facial stripes; the stripes on the body end at a reddish rump. It runs with its bushy tail held straight up.

Coyotes (*Canis latrans*) look like medium-sized dogs, typically gray or reddish-gray with whitish throat and belly. The nose is more pointed and the tail bushier than most dogs, however. They are nocturnal, so listen at night for a series of high-pitched yaps. Coyotes are relative newcomers to MDI; they first appeared in the early 1980s. Park researchers do not know how many coyotes reside on the island.

White-tailed deer (*Odocoileus virginianus*) are the only deer you'll see on MDI. Although they are fairly shy and elusive, you might see deer in open meadows just before dusk. In summer, the body is reddish, and the large tail is white underneath. Fawns are spotted, with the tail again white beneath. In winter, the color is more blue-gray. Cedar foliage is a favored winter food; notice the clear browse line on cedar trees around the edges of many lakes and ponds.

Foxes (*Vulpes fulva*) are seen with many color variations, but most are reddish-yellow, darkest on the back and white on the belly. The tails of these small, dog-sized mammals are mixed with black hairs and tipped with white; the feet are black. They are most active at night and early in the morning—hunting for food that ranges from mice and hares to insects and berries. Although fairly common on MDI, they are only occasionally seen, usually along roadsides or in open meadows.

Snowshoe hare (*Lepus americanus*), also called a varying hare because the coat changes from white in winter to dark brown in summer to help it blend with the environment. These rabbitlike animals are nocturnal—look for them in your headlight beams along the roadside.

Raccoons (*Procyon lotor*) are common on the island, and probably most often seen in the evenings at campgrounds, where they raid trash cans. The natural feeding area of this omnivore is along streams and lake shores, where they wash their food before eating it. An adult typically weighs 12 to 35 pounds and is easily distinguished by the black mask over the eyes and rings on the tail.

Red Squirrel (*Tamiasciurus hudsonicus*), sometimes called the spruce squirrel because it is common in the island's spruce-fir forests. About 7 to 8 inches long, its upper parts are reddish or yellowish and the belly is white. In summer, a black line is visible along its side. Listen for its noisy chatter; it is active all year. An individual squirrel has a home range of less than 200 yards.

Long-tail weasels (*Mustela frenata*) are long, slender animals you might see near water. In summer, they are rich brown with a white belly and a black tip on the tail. In winter, they turn white except for the black on the tail. They are shy animals and chiefly nocturnal, so a brief glimpse is all that might be expected. These weasels are sometimes confused with **MINK** (*Mustela vison*), but mink are uniformly dark brown.

Common Coastal Birds

MDI is home to an astonishing diversity of birds and is a popular destination for bird-watching enthusiasts. A checklist of birds in Acadia National Park lists 326 species present at some time over the years, either as summer or winter residents, transients, or rare visitors. The coast is a particularly good place to observe birds—there are no obstructing trees, and all the birds you see can be identified as members of only a few families or groups. Forest species are more numerous and more difficult to identify. This guide provides only a quick look at some of the most common birds you might see along the island's coast and in its forests.

Bald eagles (*Haliaetus leucocephalus*) can be seen all year on MDI. At 30 inches long and with a wingspan reaching 7 feet, this is the largest bird on the island. The stark white head gives the bird its name, and with its deep brown body and stark white tail it is impressive both in flight and when it rests atop high trees. The beak and feet are yellow. It eats mostly fish and carrion, sometimes stealing its meals from osprey. Eagles are often sighted near the small islands of Frenchman Bay, which are important nesting sites for them. Never approach an eagle's nest, especially from early spring to midsummer, as you might cause the adult to leave or prevent its return.

Black guillemots (*Cepphus grylle*) are of the family of birds known as auks, which are oceanic birds that return to land only to breed. They are expert swimmers and divers, and use their wings to swim underwater in pursuit of fish and small crustaceans. Also known as sea pigeons, they are common along the Maine coast and are usually seen floating on the sea. About 13 inches long, they are smaller than any ocean duck in the area. In spring and summer the color pattern is distinctive: the bird is totally black except for a large, white patch on each wing and bright red feet and legs that show when the bird is flying.

Double-crested cormorants (*Phalacrocorax auritus*) are common along the Maine coast during spring, summer, and fall. This large, heavy-bodied, black bird is often conspicuously perched on a buoy or rocky ledge with its wings hanging spread out to its sides. Unlike many other water birds, the cormorant does not produce enough oil to keep its feathers water resistant, so periodic sessions drying out in the sun are common. This lack of oil has a benefit—it improves the bird's diving capabilities. Cormorants

Double-crested cormorants

can dive 40 to 50 feet underwater and were once used in the Orient for fishing. Cormorants stand upright, with a curved neck and a long, slender bill with a hook at the tip. They fly low and somewhat awkwardly over the water, singly or in flocks. When swimming on the surface, they can be confused with loons; however, the cormorant's slender bill is pointed upward at an angle.

Common eiders (*Somateria mollissima*) are most conspic-uous in winter, when great rafts of eiders congregate in the rough seas. The common eider is the largest duck in Maine, about 25 inches long. The male has a white back, black belly, and black on the top of its head. The bill is yellow. The female is a large, brown duck with a low pro-file and a flat forehead. Eiders are diving ducks that subsist largely on blue mussels swallowed whole. They also eat small shellfish, crabs, shrimp, urchins, and some fish. Now common, few eiders remained as recently as 80 years ago because of pressures from hunters and egg collectors.

Herring gulls (*Larus argentatus*) are extremely common throughout the Northern Hemisphere, although at the turn of the century the species was endangered because of over-harvesting for feathers. It is a large bird (about 24 inches long). Adults are white except for a gray mantle across the wings and back and black tips on the wings. Their legs are flesh colored. The heavy, yellow bill has a distinctive red spot near the tip. Immature herring gulls are dark brown during the first year, growing lighter until adult plumage is reached in the fourth year. Herring gulls make loud, rau-cous cries. They are aggressive predators, eating the eggs and young of terns, ducks, cormorants, and other birds.

They sometimes drop shells from the air to break them open to obtain the meat inside.

Great black-backed gulls (*Larus marinus*) are common to the Maine coast. They are slightly larger (about 30 inches long) than herring gulls, and they are dominant when both are present. This species is easily recognized by its large size and the black mantle across the wings and back. The rest of the body is white, except for a yellow bill with a red dot near the tip and flesh-colored legs. Like the herring gull, this species is an aggressive predator.

Great blue herons (*Ardea herodias*), at 4 feet tall with a 6-foot wingspan, are also one of the largest birds to be seen along the Maine coast, and also one of the most distinctive. Its blue-gray color is striking, and its long legs, upright posture and long, curved neck are unmistakable. The head is mostly white with a broad, black streak running through the eye and finishing in a shaggy crest. Its bill is long, yellow, and sharply pointed. Herons nest in colonies and in trees, and feed in nearby tidal mud flats, open salt marshes, or freshwater ponds and marshes. They eat small fish, eels, crustaceans, frogs, snakes, mice, and insects. Heron are relatively abundant on MDI from April through October, but canoeists have the best chance of seeing them in places like Bass Harbor Marsh.

Common loons (*Gavia immer*) are part of the Maine mystique—the haunting call, echoing over water, can send a chill down your spine. This is a large, goose-sized bird (about 32 inches long) that spends the cold months at sea and returns to the island's lakes and ponds to breed as soon as the ice has cleared. Its spring and summer breeding plumage is distinctive: a black head with straight, stout bill and vibrant red eye; a white-and-black checkered back, white breast, and a broken white-striped neck. During the rest of the year, the straight, gray bill is the best identification. Loons are diving birds, known to have reached depths of 200 feet, and if you paddle MDI's lakes you'll be startled at how quickly they can vanish and how far they swim before returning to the surface. Loons eat fish, shellfish, crustaceans, frogs, and insects. They are clumsy on land—their legs are located far back on their bodies, which gives them great power underwater but poor balance on shore. As a result, their nests are typically quite close to water's edge, and boaters should be careful not to disturb them. In the air, they are strong, fast fliers.

Common loon

Osprey (*Pandion haliaetus*), also called fish hawks, are large birds, about 24 inches long and with a wingspan reaching up to 6 feet. The white head has a broad, black stripe running from before the eye down the neck to the back; the breast is white, while the top of its wings and back are dark brown. In flight, the wings have a characteristic backward angle at the wrist. Osprey will soar 30 to 100 feet over the ocean in search of fish—then drop suddenly, wings slightly folded, and plummet feet first into the water to sink their sharp talons into a fish. Their talons have a sandpapery bottom that helps the bird grip slippery prey. Now common along the Maine coast from mid-April through September, osprey were rare only 30 years ago when populations dwindled because of problems caused

Osprey

by DDT and other environmental contaminants. They are still an endangered species, although current populations are stable. MDI has a few prominent nests—huge accumulations of branches set high on a cliff or tree that grow larger and more complex with repeated use over the years by the same breeding pair. Do not disturb osprey nests.

Semipalmated plover (*Charadrius semipalmatus*) is one variety of plover that might be seen on the island's beaches, mud flats, and shallow, open marshes. The semipalmated plover is a small, plump bird with a brown back and a single, wide, dark ring across its white breast. It is a quick, active bird, about 7 inches long; much smaller than the similar-looking killdeer. The name semipalmated refers to partially webbed toes that help support it on mud. Look for these birds on mud flats or a sandy beach at low tide, where they feed on tiny crustaceans, worms, mollusks, and marine insects.

Sanderlings (*Calidris alba*) are great fun to watch as they dash back and forth on the beach, first seemingly being chased by the incoming waves, then darting back as the waves retreat in search of tiny particles of food. These are small (8 inches long), pale sandpipers, with a white chest, pale gray back, and a dark mark on the shoulder. The bill and legs are black, and when it flies it shows a bold white stripe along the gray-and-black wing. You are most likely to see this species in late summer or fall.

Common terns (*Sterna hirundo*) are slender, graceful birds, about 15 inches long and with a distinctive, forked tail. The body and tail are white; the head is white with a delicate black cap and a red-orange bill with black tip.

The legs and feet are orange-red. Sometimes called sea swallows, they fly with deep wing beats and often hover over the surface before dropping to make a quick, shallow dive into the water for small fish and shrimp. Terns were almost exterminated during the late 1800s by feather hunters. Terns are not common on MDI—they are more likely to be seen off the coast on small outer islands, where they breed. Boaters should be cautious in nesting areas; if the adults are startled into flight, the eggs and chicks are easy prey for gulls.

Greater and **lesser yellowlegs** (*Tringa melanoleuca* and *Tringa flavipes*) are other examples of MDI's shore birds. The lesser yellowlegs is about 10 inches long, large among the sandpipers seen on the island but noticeably smaller than the greater yellowlegs. The lesser yellowlegs has a slender, gray-and-white body; long, yellow legs; and a long, dark, straight bill. The greater yellowlegs is large (about 14 inches long) with color and shape essentially the same, except that the dark bill of the greater is heavier, longer, and slightly upturned. Both are typically seen wading in the shallow water of mud flats or in open marshes. When flying, both show a dark wing, a white rump, a light tail, and yellow feet hanging out behind. The call is the best way to distinguish between the two yellowlegs—the lesser has only one or two notes ("yew" or "yu-yu"), while the greater has a loud three- or four-note call ("whew-whew-whew").

Common Inland Birds
Black-capped chickadees (*Parus atricapillus*) are a delightful part of MDI's landscape. These small (4 to 5

Black-capped chickadee

inches long), gray birds are easily identified by their black cap, black bib, and white cheeks. They are smaller than sparrows, with longer tails and small stubby bills. These are active, often amusing birds to watch as they do acrobatics in search of food. The call is distinctive, even to novice birders: "chick-a-dee-dee-dee" or a shortened "dee-dee-dee." This is the Maine state bird.

Peregrine falcons (*Falco peregrinus*) show the classic look of falcons—long, pointed wings and long, narrow tails. The wing strokes are rapid, and the slim wings are best for speed, not sustained soaring. About the size of a crow, adults have a slate-gray back and bars on the belly; immature birds are browner, with heavy streaking on the breast. These birds are fierce aerial hunters. Peregrines are an endangered species; their populations were decimated by the effects of pesticides in the 1950s and 1960s. Acadia is one of several national parks where attempts to restore the species are underway. Young falcons have been raised and released from hack boxes high in the cliffs of Champlain Mountain. The Precipice Trail, one of Acadia's most famous because of the old iron ladders necessary to assist hikers up the steep cliffs, has been closed at certain times in recent years because peregrines nest nearby. If it's closed during your visit, check the trail descriptions in this book or ask a ranger for information about other ladder trails in the park.

Ruffed grouse (*Bonasa umbellus*) are rarely seen unless one springs into the air, wings pounding, when your footsteps tread too near. They are large (16 to 19 inches long), chickenlike birds, generally a mottled red-brown or gray-brown. The fan-shaped tail has a broad, black band near the tip. Those distant chain saws you hear, by the way, are the drumming of the male; the booming starts slowly, then builds to a whir: "bup...bup...bup...bup bup bup rrrrr."

Red-breasted nuthatches (*Sitta canadensis*) are small, chubby, tree-climbing birds. Smaller than sparrows, they have rusty-colored breasts and a broad, black line through the eye. This species prefers evergreens. Nuthatches are the only tree climbers that go down tree trunks head first. The red-breasted nuthatch is quite similar to the white-breasted, although the latter has no eye stripe and has a white breast.

Oven birds (*Seiurus aurocapillus*) are small, sparrow-sized birds that favor deciduous woodlands. They build their nests among the leaves on the forest floor and are

Images of Acadia

Otter cliffs at sunrise. Lou Lainey

Above: Rhodora in bloom at Eagle Lake. Tammis Coffin/Friends of Acadia

Below: October leaves along the carriage road near Little Long Pond in Seal Harbor. Earl Brechlin

Above: Summer solitude on a misty day at Sand Beach. Tammis Coffin/ Friends of Acadia

Below: Cross country skiers on a carriage road near Eagle Lake. Earl Brechlin

Above: A porcupine nibbles on bark at the foot of Champlain Mountain. Lou Lainey

Left: Lupine flourishes in fields along the ocean at Compass Harbor. Earl Brechlin

Evidence of beaver near Bar Harbor. Lou Lainey

Clockwise from right: Hikers on the trail to Sargent Mountain Pond (Earl Brechlin); children at play on the shore of Jordan Pond (Tammis Coffin); sailboats in Northeast Harbor (Earl Brechlin).

Above: The Beehive.
Earl Brechlin

Left: An iron ladder on the Beech Cliff Trail.
Earl Brechlin

Swollen with runoff from an evening rain, Hadlock Brook cascades over ledges along a carriage road. Earl Brechlin

sometimes seen walking along the ground or logs on their pale, pinkish legs. Their appearance is thrushlike, olive-brown above and striped, rather than spotted, below. At close range, an orange patch is visible on the top of the head, but such a sighting would be uncommon as oven birds are heard far more than seen. The song is an emphatic "teacher, teacher, TEACHER," repeated rapidly over and over, growing louder with each repetition.

Ravens (*Corvus corax*) are large (21 to 26 inches long) black birds, about twice the size of a crow, for which they are often mistaken. Ravens are more hawklike in flight, flapping their wings and soaring on horizontal wings. In flight, the tail from below appears wedge shaped; if perched nearby, look for shaggy throat feathers. Habit gives another clue: crows tend to flock, while ravens are more solitary. Ravens "croak" rather than "caw." They feed mostly on carrion, and prefer the less-developed parts of the island.

White-throated sparrows (*Zonotrichia albicollis*) are small (6 to 7 inches long), gray-breasted birds with a white throat patch and a striped black-and-white crown. There is a yellow spot between the bill and eye. Its song is a series of clear, pensive whistles, often interpreted as "Old Sam Peabody, Peabody, Peabody."

Scarlet tananger (*Piranga olivacea*), one of MDI's most stunning birds, arrives in late May. This vivid bird is scarlet with black wings and tail, 6 1/2 to 7 1/2 inches long. It frequents old-growth forest stands, and can be conspicuous from great distances because of the color.

Warblers, such as the **Myrtle** (*Dendroica coronata coronata*) and **Black-throated green** (*Dendroica virens*), bring a great variety of color and song to MDI. Myrtle warblers have a distinctive yellow rump and white throat; they arrive early in spring, just past mid-April, and are common on the island. Black-throated green warblers have an olive-green back, black throat, and yellow cheeks. The call is a lisping "zoo zee zoo zoo zee" or "zee zee zee zee zoo zee."

Cedar waxwings (*Bombycilla cedrorum*) enliven MDI's forests in summer with their thin, lisping "zeee" calls. This is a sleek, crested, brown bird with a broad, yellow band at the tip of the tail and a banditlike mask across the eyes. The crest gives it a cardinal-like appearance.

Downy woodpeckers (*Dendrocopus pubescens*) are relatively small woodpeckers (6 to 7 inches long), with a white breast and checkered black-and-white back. It is one of only two species with a white back (the other being the hairy woodpecker, a similar but slightly larger species). Males have a small, red patch on the back of the head.

Pileated woodpeckers (*Hylatomus pileatus*) announce their presence with powerful hammering that can echo through MDI's deciduous forests. Look for the deep, oblong or almost square holes they carve in search of insects. This is a large (17 to 19 inches long), shy woodpecker with a distinctive red crest. The body is black; the face and neck are striped black and white.

Reptiles, Amphibians, & Insects

Reptiles and amphibians are cold-blooded animals, deriving heat from outside sources and controlling their body temperatures by moving to cooler or warmer environments as necessary. MDI, with its cool climate, is not an ideal habitat for them. However, enough species of two classes live on the island to add another layer of diversity to it's life. Reptiles are covered in scales, shields, or other plating and have claws on their toes. Amphibians have moist, glandular skin and their toes are devoid of claws—and importantly, they spend part of their life cycle in the water. To observe either class, you'll have to watch carefully, for most species are shy and secretive. All species found on the island are nonpoisonous.

Insects, here on MDI as everywhere, show a staggering diversity of form and habit. There are more kinds of insects known than all other animals visible to the naked eye— 900,000 species have been identified so far. Related to crabs and lobsters, insects carry their skeleton on the outside of their body, which has three sections (head, thorax, and abdomen) and six legs, with some exceptions. The island is also home to some insectlike animals that are often confused with insects. For example, spiders have only two body divisions, four pairs of legs, and no antennae. Centipedes and millipedes have many body segments with one or two pair of legs on each. Insects and their relatives play an important role in nature—they are food for many kinds of fish, amphibians, birds, and mammals. Few visitors keep a life list of insects, the way birdwatchers do of birds, yet they can be fascinating. As with all wildlife watching, the key is careful observation.

REPTILES

Eastern garter snakes (*Thamnophis sirtalis sirtalis*) are black, dark brown, green, or olive colored, about 1 to 2 feet long, with three distinct lateral strips in varied colors, from greenish to yellowish to brown. This common snake is found in many habitats on MDI, including meadows, marshes, and woodlands. It is often seen along trails and carriage roads in the summer.

Eastern milk snakes (*Lampropeltis triangulum triangulum*) are somewhat slender, gray or tannish snakes, with several rows of brown or reddish-brown patches down the body. The camouflage works well in woodlands. They are 2 to 3 feet long and bear a slight resemblance to the copperhead, but remember that MDI has no poisonous snakes.

Eastern smooth green snakes (*Opheodrys nernalis*), sometimes called grass snakes, are shy snakes, bright green above and plain white or washed with yellow below. They are about 1 to 1 1/2 feet long, with smooth scales.

Snapping turtles (*Chelydra serpentina*) have been described as ugly, both in appearance and disposition. This turtle has a large head, a rather flat shell (carapace), and a long tail. Its color varies from almost black to brown, and it usually grows to about 8 to 12 inches. These strong swimmers are abundant in the island's ponds, lakes, and marshes. As their name implies, they can inflict a painful bite.

Eastern painted turtles (*Chrysemys picta picta*) are best identified by their smooth shells with patterns of red, yellow, and black along the margins. They grow to be 5 or 6 inches long. Look for bright yellow spots on the head.

These turtles prefer shallower water—beaver ponds, for instance—and groups are often seen basking on logs.

AMPHIBIANS

Green frogs (*Rana clamitans melanota*) are abundant wherever there is shallow fresh water—lake shore, streams, ponds, even drainage ditches. Their color varies greatly from bold green to greenish-brown, with dark blotches. They are about 2 to 3 1/2 inches long, with 2 distinct ridges down the back from eyes to rump. In summer, their call is an explosive croaking, sounding like a loose banjo string, either a single note or repeated 3 to 4 times.

Leopard frogs (*Rana pipiens*) are medium-sized, spotted frogs, typically brown or green with 2 to 3 rows of irregular, dark spots, round with light borders. (The **Pickerel**

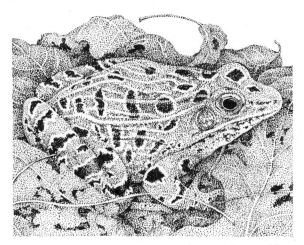

Leopard frog

frog [*Rana palustris*], for comparison, has squarish spots.) They have conspicuous ridges along the back. In summer, they may wander well away from water; their call is a deep, rattling snore interspaced with grunts.

Wood frogs (*Rana sylvatica*) are the bandits of the amphibian world—note the black mask across the eyes. Generally brown and only 1 to 2 inches long, they favor moist wooded areas and are quite secretive. The call is a hoarse clack or quack.

Spring peepers (*Hyla crucifer*) enliven spring and early summer nights with a riotous chorus of their high-pitched, whistlelike "preep, preep, preep." These tiny tree frogs (less than 1 inch) are rarely seen but vary from brown to gray to olive; a dark X, often imperfect, crosses the back. They are abundant in second-growth areas and near any small ponds or marshes.

Northern dusky salamanders (*Desmognathus fuscus fuscus*) seldom wander far from trickling water, but are abundant near streams where stones, chunks of wood, and other debris provide shelter. They are usually 2 1/2 to 4 1/2 inches long, and their tail takes up almost half their total length. Skin color varies, but gray or brown (similar to the ground color) is common.

Red-backed salamanders (*Plethodon cinereus cinereus*) grow to 2 to 4 inches in length and are best identified by the straight-edged, reddish stripe from the base of the head to the tail. This common terrestrial salamander lives in wooded areas.

Tiger swallowtail

INSECTS

Butterflies are plentiful in summer. They usually fly by day and rest with their wings folded back. You might see **Tiger swallowtails** (*Papilio glaucus*), large, striking butterflies with a 4-to-5-inch wingspread and pale yellow wings with bold, black markings and border; **Monarchs** (*Danaus plexippus*), which migrate incredible distances, are 3 to 4 inches across with rounded, deep red-orange wings patterned with black veins and white-dotted black borders; sulphurs, either the **Clouded sulphur** or **Orange sulphur** (*Colias philodice* or *Colias eurytheme*), which are 1 to 2 inches across, generally pale yellow, and common in meadows and grassy roadsides; or **Common blues** (*Lycaenopsis argiolus*), tiny butterflies—about 1 inch across—abundant in open deciduous woods.

Dragonflies and **damselflies** are both powerful fliers that zip about near water in search of prey. Dragonflies are larger and rest with their wings outstretched. Damselflies are more delicate and rest with wings folded over their backs.

Fireflies are not flies at all but soft-bodied beetles. The flash you see is a call for a mate. The females generally sit on the ground or vegetation and flash in response to males. The flash pattern is specific to each species. Their larvae, found in moist soil and rotting organic material, also glow.

Moths also are common. They usually fly at night and rest with their wings open; their antennae are often feathery. Common species include **Cecropia moths** (*Nyalaphora cecropia*), with a wingspread of 4 to 6 inches and a prominent, crescent-shaped eye spot on each brown wing; **Luna moths** (*Actias luna*), attractive, pale green moths about 3 to 4 inches across; and **Polyphemus moths** (*Antheraea polyphemus*), with their velvety wings in shades of yellow, brown, and rust.

Water boatman is common in ponds and streams all around the island. The name refers to the oarlike rowing motions of its legs as it moves through the water in search of plant debris or algae.

Water striders are remarkably adapted to life on the water's surface, taking advantage of surface tension to stay afloat. These predators skate along the surface attacking other insects.

Ocean Life

Acadia National Park encompasses 44 miles of rocky, undeveloped shorelines. Most are rugged—boulder beaches, tidal pools, and rocky cliffs. Yet life abounds in the intertidal zone, the stretch of coast that is under water at high tide but above the sea's reach at low tide. This is one of the earth's most complex and demanding environments: Living things must be adapted to the twice-daily rise and fall of the tides (an 8-to-10-foot rise is typical here). They must be able to survive exposure to the air, extremes of heat and cold, changes in salinity and oxygen availability, and the powerful pounding of the surf.

When the tide retreats, pools of sea water—tidepools—are left behind. These temporarily isolated habitats reflect the great diversity of marine life. They shelter sea stars, periwinkles, anemones, crabs, and many other marine invertebrates, as well as many species of plants, each specifically adapted to its particular niche. One animal or plant, for example, might be adapted to tolerate a 6-hour exposure to air, but 8 hours might be fatal. As a result, each organism's tolerance to exposure determines its location within the tidal zone. Although it's fun to handle tidepool species to get a closer look, please return them promptly to the same place you found them. *Never* take samples with you—they'll die and you'll be preventing other visitors from experiencing the abundance and variety of tidepool life.

In your explorations, moving from the land toward the sea, you will see three sometimes overlapping bands of life.

The *splash zone* is highest on the shore, marked by a characteristic, irregular black band of blue-green algae and abundant tiny periwinkles tucked among the crevices.

The true *intertidal zone* is the midtide area, from a whitish belt of abundant barnacles that marks the upper limit of normal high tide to deeper areas with many seaweeds. Species here are able to withstand exposure to air to varying degrees during the tidal cycle. Within this zone, there are subzones often called the barnacle, rockweed, red-green algae, and kelp zones, with the organisms in each zone progressively less able to withstand exposure to the air.

The *subtidal zone*, the deepest parts of a tidepool, is where organisms can tolerate only limited exposure to the air.

Beyond the tidal zone, the ocean is home to many deep-water species of fish, plants, and animals that visitors rarely see. There are lobsters, of course, but we see those mostly on dinner plates. Of special interest to many visitors are the marine mammals, some of which are fairly common off MDI's coast. A boat trip, whether with a commercial operator or a National Park Service naturalist, can add a unique dimension to your stay. Here is a sampling of the species you might encounter while exploring Acadia, MDI, and nearby harbors, bays, and islands.

Common Seaweeds

Corallina (*Corallina officinalis*), also called coral weed, is a delicate, many-branched seaweed that grows 1 or 2 inches tall. Ranging in color from pinkish-white to deep purple, this red alga has the ability to precipitate calcium and magnesium carbonate on itself, which gives it a hard, corallike appearance. It grows in the deeper areas of the intertidal zone and in the subtidal zone.

Dulse (*Rhodymeria palmata*) is a thick, almost rubbery-looking red seaweed that grows near the low-tide mark. You'll often see solitary plants of this edible seaweed, which is sometimes harvested, dried, and sold in health-food stores.

Irish moss (*Chondrus crispus*), despite the name, is a red alga. This seaweed varies in color from deep red to brown, and grows in dense, carpetlike clumps. It is often found in exposed parts of tidepools. It's best known as a source of carrageenan, a natural thickening agent sometimes used in ice cream, toothpaste, paint, and other products.

Kelps are large, leathery, brown seaweeds typical of deeper water but sometimes found just at or below the low-tide mark. Look for a distinctive attachment—strong, almost fingerlike roots that give the plant an extremely strong but flexible grip to the bottom. *Laminaria saccharina* has a single, elongated blade. **Horsetail kelp** (*Laminaria digitata*) is similar, but with a wider blade and divided lengthwise. **Winged kelp** (*Alaria esculenta)* has 1 long, narrow, main blade with a distinct central midrib.

Laver (*Phorphyra sps.*) is a thin, delicate seaweed—almost tissuelike. It ranges in color from red to light purple to olive green; it is often used in soups in the Orient.

Sea lettuce (*Ulva lactuca*) is a common, bright green seaweed (a green alga, actually) with delicate, very thin, wavy green leaves—just like leaf lettuce. It grows in small clumps.

Bladder wrack (*Fucus vesiculosis*), also called rockweed, is a brown alga with broad, flat blades that break repeatedly into Y-shaped forks. Distinctive midribs and air

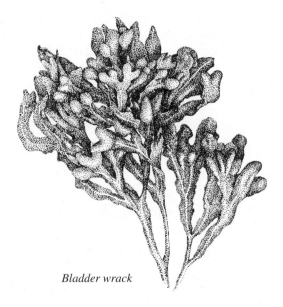

Bladder wrack

bladders are in pairs on flat wings. It's usually found high in the intertidal zone.

Knotted wrack (*Ascophyllum nodosum*) is a stringy, large seaweed, a brown alga that is usually olive colored, rubbery, with float bladders at irregular intervals along the main axis and principal branches.

Common Tidepool Animals

Rock barnacles (*Balanus balanoides*) are so common that the whitish band high in the intertidal zone is often called the barnacle zone. These tiny, armored creatures hardly look alive—they look more like miniature volcanoes—but they are crustaceans related to lobsters and crabs. They start life in the spring as tiny, swimming larvae; they find a place to settle and, secreting a glue that is one of the strongest known, attach permanently to some surface—it could be a rock or a boat hull. At low tide, barnacles are inactive and their shells close to conserve moisture. To observe them in action, find some in a shallow tidepool and gently stir the water to mimic the incoming tide. The creature's shell should open and an array of feathery appendages will wave gracefully in the water, searching for food.

Green crabs (*Carcinus maenas*) are small (1 to 3 inches long), feisty crabs often found hidden in the rockweed. They have long, pointy walking legs (the last leg is not modified for swimming as in many crabs), and can move very fast when provoked. They are sometimes called little green meanies, so beware your fingers if you try to capture one; although their pincers are small, they can give you a nasty pinch.

Hermit crabs (*Pagurus acadianus*) do not have a hard, outer shell (carapace) to protect their soft organs, so they rely instead on finding discarded shells in which to live. As they grow, they must find larger shells to occupy. Often found in periwinkle shells, these are scavengers found throughout the intertidal area. The claws are reddish and the eye stalks are bluish.

Rock crabs (*Cancer irroratus*) are common, shallow-water crabs that sometimes can be found in tidepools. The shell is oval, 3 to 4 inches across, brown or yellowish, with 9 wide, smooth marginal teeth along the sides of the cara-pace (shell). Check the underside to determine sex: on males, the abdomen is a narrow, isosceles triangle; on females, the triangle is broad, more equilateral.

Limpets (*Acmaea sps.*), sometimes called Chinaman's hat snail, is the only limpet common on MDI. Its shell is a gentle cone, round to oblong, and typically gray or brownish. It prefers cool water, and attaches to rocks with surprising strength—be careful if you attempt to remove one that you don't injure the limpet. It feeds on algae on rock surfaces using its rasplike radula, or tooth.

American lobster (*Homarus americanus*) or Maine lobster, as it is sometimes called, is a mottled brown or greenish black, with a distinctive first pair of legs, usually called claws, and 3 pairs of walking legs with pincers. The left first claw is usually larger, with blunt, rounded teeth, while the right has smaller pincers and sharp, pointed teeth. The tail ends in 5 flat panels, while underneath are feathery swimmerets. It is rare to find large lobsters in tidepools, but you may find 2 to 3 inch juveniles in late spring or early summer.

Blue mussels (*Mytilus edulis*) inhabit the middle range of the intertidal zone, where they sometimes form thick beds. The smooth shell of this bivalve is shiny blue or almost black; they attach to rocks with strong byssal threads. They feed when the tide comes in carrying its abundance of microscopic life—the 2 sides of the shell separate and water flows in, carrying food and oxygen.

Common periwinkles (*Littorina litorea*) are hardy creatures, able to withstand periods without food or water. They are generally found in the splash zone or high in the midtide zone, clinging to rocks or tucked in crevices. They are vegetarians that graze algae from rock surfaces with a raspy, tonguelike radula; they breathe air and bear live young. These snails are usually dark brown and have 6 or 7 gentle whorls in the spire of their shell; the head and foot are dark gray and the sole of the foot is cream colored. A related species, the smooth or **Northern periwinkle** (*Littorina obtusata*) is yellow or bright orange, smaller, and commonly found on rockweed and other large algae near the low-tide line, where they stay hidden in the wet seaweeds because they can withstand only brief exposure to the air.

Sea cucumber (*Cucumaria frondosa*) is another unlikely-looking relative of the starfish. This echinoderm also has 5 segments, but they are harder to see in this soft, leathery animal. The body is elongated like a cucumber, perhaps up to 10 inches, and there are tube feet arranged in 5 longitudinal tracts that enable the creature to move about slowly. The color is reddish-brown, lighter underneath. When feeding, long, treelike tentacles extend from the tip; when violently disturbed, the animal will contract its body so powerfully that it will eject much of its internal organs. If the damage is not extensive, these will regenerate. Sea cucumbers are common below the low-tide line, but are sometimes found stranded in tidepools.

Blood star (*Henricia sanguinolenta*), when found in the intertidal zone, is a small (2 to 4 inches long), deeply colored sea star, with shades ranging from blood red to orange, purple, rose, or cream. Its surface is smoother than the purple star's.

Daisy brittle star (*Ophiopholis aculeaata*) vary greatly in color and markings. Brittle stars move relatively quickly by starfish standards, using flexible arms attached to a central disk rather than tube feet. As with all starfish, if the brittle star loses 1 or more of its 5 arms, the arms simply grow back.

Purple sea star (*Asterias vulgaris*), also called northern or common star, is the most common starfish (6 to 12 inches long) along the Maine coast. Look for 5 arms (a clue to all the echinoderms, a family that includes sea stars, urchins, and other 5-segmented organisms); rough, spiny skin that varies from purple to pink to orange; and rows of tube feet under each arm that allow the animal to move and grip prey. They often feed on mussels by wrapping around the shell, exerting tremendous strength to force the shell apart, then everting their stomachs through their mouths to envelop and ingest the food.

Green sea urchin (*Strongylocentrotus droebachiensis*) is the only urchin north of Cape Cod, a pin-cushionlike creature with light green spines. Common in shallow ocean water (30 to 60 feet deep), in the intertidal zone they are found in tidepools hidden in deep crevices or around boulders. When submerged, they may show long, dark, tube feet extended beyond the spines searching for food. Urchins are scavengers that feed on living and dead plants and animals; they have a chewing apparatus called Aristotle's lantern, fine, bony plates ending in a circle of sharp teeth that protrude from a small hole in the center of the animal's underside. You may find urchin shells (or tests) well up on shore, where gulls have dropped them in an

Green sea urchin

attempt to break them open. Note the 5 sections of the shell; this is another echinoderm.

Dog whelks (*Thais lapillus*) are predatory snails—the carnivores of the island's snails. Common in the intertidal zone, they feed on barnacles, mussels, and periwinkles. You can identify the dog whelk by the small notch in the shell, from which comes a drill—a long, toothed radula used to make holes in the shells of other animals. After drilling a hole, the whelk simply sucks out the soft parts of its prey. A whelk shell has 5 or 6 whorls; color varies with diet, and can be brown, white, yellow, orange, and purple, with various patterns of stripes. In summer, you may find egg capsules—tiny, ricelike grains—attached to the underside of flat rocks.

Marine Mammals

Gray seals (*Halichoerus grypus*) are larger than harbor seals, a male growing up to 8 feet and weighing 800 pounds, and far less common around MDI. The face differs as well: there is a distinctive Roman nose and gaping nostrils that become pronounced with age. (The scientific name translates as "hooknosed pig of the sea.") The color pattern is generally bolder and more coarsely spotted than in harbor seals.

Harbor seals (*Phoca vitulina concolor*) are the most common seals in the waters surrounding MDI. Typically 5 to 6 feet in length, this sleek, bewhiskered seal ranges from light gray or tan to brown, black, or even reddish, with fine, dark mottling or spots. To some, this is known as the sea dog, as when bobbing in the sea the animal's profile shows a short muzzle and a concave forehead like that of a cocker spaniel. A male may weigh 200 pounds. This seal forages during high tide; during low tide, it often is seen basking on coastal islands and ledges. During the late

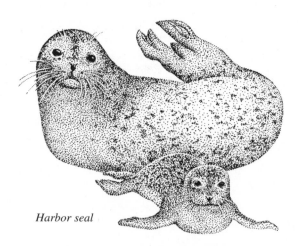

Harbor seal

1800s there was a bounty on harbor seals in an attempt to reduce seal populations and, in turn, increase the fish caught by humans. They were nearly exterminated in certain areas by the early 1900s, but populations have rebounded, in part because they are protected under the 1972 Marine Mammals Act. Boaters should be cautious not to approach too closely; when seals on ledges lift their heads or act nervous, retreat.

Harbor porpoises (*Phocoena phocoena*) are common in the bays and open ocean around MDI. Ranging in size from 4 to 6 feet, they are most easily seen on calm days, when they show a triangular dorsal fin as they surface to breathe. There is no visible spout, but you may hear a soft puffing sound when they exhale. They are pale gray on the flanks, and darker gray on the rest of the body. Harbor porpoises are among the smallest of the toothed whales, and will venture close to shore and into harbors in pursuit of fish. During early spring, harbor porpoises appear individually or in small, loose groups. Later, from August through September, larger groups of 20 or more are sometimes seen.

Harbor porpoise

Whales are among the most impressive of all animals, and while not a common part of a visitor's experience on MDI, they can be seen on boat trips, especially trips out toward the Georges Bank. **Finback Whales** (*Balaenoptera physalus*) are most common—these are huge, sleek animals, reaching 60 to 70 feet in length and weighing 50 to 60 tons. This is a baleen whale (toothless whales that feed by filtering food from the sea through plates of baleen in their mouths); their behavior is not as acrobatic as that of some species, but their size inspires awe. They can be spotted from a distance by their robust spouts, which can rise up to 20 feet, and the appearance of prominent back and dorsal fins. Less common off the island are **Minke whales** (*Balaenoptera acutorostrata*), baleen whales about 15 to 30 feet long, and **Humpback whales** (*Megaptera novaeangliae*), baleen whales (30 to 60 feet long) known for leaping out of the water (breaching) and other impressive behavior displays.

Trails

A CADIA NATIONAL PARK offers some of the best
hiking and walking opportunities in the United States.
More than 100 mi. of maintained and marked trails provide
a unique network of mountain, lake shore, and seaside
paths. A 57-mi. system of carriage roads, barred to automobiles, permits pleasant walking, bicycling, easy snowshoe-
ing and cross-country ski routes, and clear horseback trails.
The National Park Service (NPS) encourages their use. The
fine-grained gravel surface on the carriage roads around
Eagle Lake and Witch Hole Pond makes them suitable for
bicycles with small-diameter tires. Other carriage roads tend
to have a softer, looser surface suitable for non-motorized
mountain bikes. Bicycles (including mountain bicycles),
however, are not allowed on any hiking trails within the
park. The descriptions within this guide are limited to trails
reserved only for hiking, and so do not cover the carriage
roads. However, the carriage roads are marked on the map.

The traveler on Mount Desert Island should be prepared for the changeable weather of the northern New
England seashore. Changes can be swift, but because the
maximum elevation, Cadillac Mountain, is only 1530 ft.,

problems will generally involve discomfort and not danger. These trails are all within a few miles of roads or houses. The terrain is often sharp and precipitous, so the climber who explores off marked trails risks uncomfortable going and even dead ends at cliffs and ravines. The hiker can find paths of any desired degree of difficulty, from the mildest lakeside paths to challenging "ladder" trails with iron rungs driven into rock as the tread. (Novice hikers should consult a park ranger for specific advice on how difficult a trail to attempt.) Most of the summits are treeless and open. Trails on MDI's treeless peaks often have rock cairns to guide hikers. In the event of heavy fog, the hiker must make certain to locate the next cairn before leaving the last when above treeline. Also, in the colder months trails may be covered with ice. Check with the park visitor center for current conditions.

There are NPS camping facilities inside the National Park. A complete selection of hotels, motels, tourist homes, and private campgrounds is also available on the island. Park campsites, shown on the map, are at Blackwoods (by reservation from June 15–Sept. 15, call 1-800-365-CAMP; first-come, first-served for the rest of the year) and Seawall (first-come, first-served from late May to late September). For detailed park campground information, write: Acadia National Park, PO Box 177, Bar Harbor ME 04609 (or phone 207-288-3338). If park campgrounds are filled, you will be referred to private campgrounds on the island. Camping in Acadia is limited to established NPS and private sites. No backcountry camping is permitted because of space limitations within the park.

Hiking, camping, and tourist information is readily available on the island. The Thompson Island Information

Center, located at the entrance to MDI, is jointly operated by the National Park Service and the island-wide Chamber of Commerce. Acadia National Park Visitor Center, on ME 3 at Hulls Cove near Bar Harbor, offers current information, including an NPS map and descriptive material. Of particular interest will be the "Acadia Beaver Log" (summer and fall only) which announces guided naturalist walks, hikes, and boat cruises. The villages of Bar Harbor, Northeast Harbor, and Southwest Harbor maintain offices that provide help to visitors.

Public excursion boats for local trips depart from the town dock areas of Bar Harbor, Northeast Harbor, Southwest Harbor, and Bass Harbor. Bar Harbor is the western terminus of a ferry (autos carried) that departs in the early morning for Yarmouth, Nova Scotia. Plan to stay overnight if you go. Round trip, this ferry makes for a long day with no appreciable time for sightseeing in Yarmouth.

Most of the larger lakes are public water supplies and thus closed to swimming, but freshwater swimming is available at a public beach, maintained by the NPS, at the south end of Echo Lake. The NPS also offers Sand Beach, a saltwater beach with fine sand and traditionally cold Maine sea bathing.

The following descriptions do not cover all the trails on the island or Acadia National Park. Some areas, around Northeast Harbor for example, are honeycombed with local woodland paths. Also, the few trails on Schoodic Peninsula, a part of Acadia National Park on the mainland north of MDI, are not covered. Those selected for detailed treatment here are well marked, offically recognized and maintained paths that give access to all of the preferred summits. For the most part, you can reach the individual summits in comfortable half-day walks. Longer or more strenuous excursions can be planned easily by including as many peaks as desired. To simplify reference and to conform with Acadia National Park nomenclature, the island is divided into an eastern district and a western district. With assistance from the AMC, Friends of Acadia, and other volunteers, the NPS maintains all trails described, and markings include signs, cairns, blue painted blazes, and metal markers. In addition to the map in this guide, refer to USGS Mount Desert and Bar Harbor quadrangles, 15-minute series.

The NPS has recently rated each trail in the park by its relative difficulty. These ratings appear on the following pages under the names of the trails. The ratings are determined by the following criteria:

Easy: Fairly level ground.

Moderate: Uneven ground with some steep grades and/or gradual climbing. Footing may be difficult in places.

Strenuous: Steep and/or long grades; steady climbing or descending. Sometimes difficult footing, difficult maneuvering.

Ladder: Iron rung ladders and handrails placed on steep grades or difficult terrain. These trails are very difficult.

These ratings are meant to guide hikers by giving a general sense of the terrain. Further, the AMC has estimated times for covering distances to help hikers plan trips. Times were calculated by allowing for $1/2$ hour for each mile of distance or 1000 ft. of climbing. Both of these systems are very limited because there is no way to account for the differences in hiker experience and pace, weather, and group size. Therefore, these times should not be relied upon as absolutes, but rather as an addition to the descriptions within this guide, which give more specific and more accurate accounts of each trail.

EASTERN DISTRICT
(East of Somes Sound)

Champlain Mountain (1058 ft./322 m.) Area

Champlain Mountain is the easternmost summit on the island. Its east face is sharp, with the Precipice Trail climbing on ladder rungs in some parts. The Bear Brook Trail offers easier access up the north ridge. From the west and the Sieur de Monts Spring area, the Beachcroft Path traverses Huguenot Head en route to the summit. To the south is the Bowl (415 ft.), a delightful mountain pond, and the Beehive (520 ft.), a sharp promontory above Sand Beach. A pleasant excursion is possible following any route up Champlain and proceeding to Sand Beach via the Bowl and the Beehive. Gorham Mountain (525 ft.) is another summit south of the Beehive.

Precipice Trail
NPS rating: Ladder

This trail starts from the Precipice Trail parking area, located 1.75 mi. beyond the Sieur de Monts Spring entrance on Park Loop Rd. at the foot of Champlain Mountain. The trailhead is located just before the park entrance fee station on Park Loop Road. This trail is not recommended for those uneasy about heights.

Following a rugged talus slope full of big boulders, the trail ascends northwest about 0.4 mi. Here, the right fork runs under the east face of the mountain to connect with the Bear Brook Trail 0.5 mi. from the summit on the north ridge. From the fork, the Precipice climbs southwest, rising steeply to a point directly west of the parking area.

The direction is now west-northwest. Along this section of the trail, ladders and iron rungs help hikers negotiate precipitous vertical drop-offs. The final 500 ft. to the summit follow gentle slopes and ledges. Hikers under 5 ft. tall may have difficulty reaching some handholds. **Caution:** It's most important that Precipice Trail hikers remain on the designated trail. Wandering off the trail can quickly lead hikers onto cliffs that require technical mountain-climbing skills and equipment.

Note: The Precipice Trail can be closed for an undetermined amount of time each spring and summer because of the reintroduction of peregrine falcons to the park. Since they are an endangered species, their nesting success is critical. The trail will thus be closed to all hikers until the falcons have established a new population. Violators of the closure are subject to a $10,000 fine. Those wishing the experience of a ladder trail should consider the nearby Beehive Trail, the Dorr Mountain Ladder Trail, the Jordan Cliffs Trail, Giant Slide Trail, or the Beech Cliffs Trail.

Precipice Trail
Distances from Park Loop Rd.
    to right fork to Bear Brook Trail: 0.4 mi., 15 min.
    to Champlain summit: 0.8 mi. (1.3 km.), 1 hr.

Bear Brook Trail
NPS rating: Moderate

This trail begins on the Park Loop Rd., 0.2 mi. east of the entrance to the Bear Brook Picnic Area. The trail ends at the northern terminus of the Gorham Mountain Trail, located at the south end of the Bowl.

This trail climbs gradually from the parking area through a mixed forest of birch, pine, and spruce to a junction on the north slope of Champlain with the Champlain East Face Trail entering left at 0.5 miles. Continuing left, the Bear Brook Trail steadily emerges from the forest canopy giving outstanding views of Frenchman Bay and Schoodic Peninsula on the mainland to the east. At 1 mile the trail reaches the open, rocky summit of Champlain. Descending, it meets the Precipice Trail, entering left at 1.1 mi., then descends into the Bowl and terminates at the Gorham Mountain Trail.

Bear Brook Trail

Distances from Park Loop Rd.

   to junction with the Champlain East Face Trail: 0.5 mi., 30 min.

   to Champlain summit: 1.0 mi., 55 min.

   to junction with the Precipice Trail: 1.1 mi., 1 hr.

   to Gorham Mt. Trail: 2.6 mi. (4.2 km.), 1 hr. 45 min.

Beachcroft Trail

NPS rating: Moderate

This is a convenient route between Champlain Mountain and the area to the west. For the most part, the trail is entirely open. While the ascent to Hugenot Head from ME 3 is gradual and easily traveled, the character of the trail becomes more difficult on the actual ascent of Champlain.

   The trail leaves ME 3 close to the north end of the Tarn and begins with a flight of granite steps on the east side of the highway. (There is parking above the north end of the Tarn off the west side of the highway.) It then runs southeast, often on carefully placed stone stairs. Following switchbacks and stone steps, it rises up and across the west face of Huguenot Head. The trail passes to the south of (not over) the summit of Huguenot Head at about 0.4 mi. A brief, gradual descent into the gully between Huguenot Head and Champlain Mountain is followed by a sharp, difficult ascent over rocks up the northwest slope of Champlain Mountain to the summit at 0.8 mi.

Beachcroft Trail

Distances from ME 3

to shoulder of Huguenot Head: 0.4 mi., 25 min.

to Champlain summit: 0.8 mi. (1.3 km.), 55 min.

Bowl Trail

NPS rating: Moderate

This trail leaves from opposite the Sand Beach parking area, located 3.25 mi. beyond Sieur de Monts Spring on the Park Loop Rd. Using this trailhead means paying an entrance fee on the Park Loop Rd.

The Bowl Trail is a gently sloping path that offers access to the Beehive Trail and the Gorham Mountain Trail. It connects Sand Beach to the Bowl, a lovely lake at the base of Halfway Mountain. At the Bowl a connector trail to the Beehive bears right.

Bowl Trail

Distances from Sand Beach Parking area

to junction with the Beehive Trail: 0.2 mi., 5 min.

to the Bowl and junction with the Beehive and Gorham
Mt. trails: 0.6 mi. (1 km.), 25 min.

Beehive Trail

NPS rating: Ladder

This trail begins 0.2 mi. up the Bowl Trail from the Sand Beach parking area. Take a sharp right at the sign marked

Beehive. For 0.3 mi., the trail rises abruptly via switch-backs and iron ladders over steep ledges to the summit of the Beehive. This trail is challenging and not for those who are uneasy on precipitous heights. The views of the French-man Bay–Sand Beach–Otter Cliff area are magnificent.

The trail continues down the northwest slope of the Beehive and dips steeply to the south for 0.2 mi. to a junction with the Gorham Mountain and Bowl trails. Take the left fork for 0.6 mi. to return to Park Loop Rd.

Beehive Trail

Distances from Park Loop Rd.

    to the Beehive: 0.5 mi., 25 min.

    to complete loop back to the Sand Beach area (via Bowl Trail): *est.* 1.3 mi. (2.1 km.), 50 min.

Gorham Mountain Trail

NPS rating: Moderate (Cadillac Cliffs Loop: Strenuous)

The trail starts at the Gorham Mountain Trail parking area (also known as the Monument Cove parking area) on Park Loop Rd. (where a user's fee is required), 1 mi. past Sand Beach. It rises gently over open ledges 0.3 mi. to a junction with the Cadillac Cliffs Trail [(NPS rating: Strenuous). The Cadillac Cliffs Trail is a loop that leads right and rejoins the Gorham Mountain Trail 0.5 mi. later, after passing under ancient sea cliffs and by an ancient sea cave.] The Gorham Mountain Trail continues 0.3 mi. over easy open granite ledges to where the Cadillac Cliffs loop rejoins the main trail.

The main trail continues north over the Gorham Mountain summit, which is open and bare, with some of the finest panoramas on Mount Desert Island. Descending, the trail reaches a junction with the Bowl Trail in another 0.7 mi. For the Bowl, go left 0.2 mi. To reach the Beehive, turn right, then left at the next junction, about 0.1 mi. farther. (Continuing straight ahead at this junction will bring you to Park Loop Rd. at Sand Beach.)

Gorham Mountain Trail

Distances from trailhead parking area

    to summit of Gorham Mt.: 1.0 mi., 45 min.

    to The Bowl: 1.7 mi., 1 hr. 5 min.

    to Park Loop Rd. in Sand Beach area: *est.* 2.3 mi. (3.7 km.), 1 hr. 30 min.

Great Head Trail

NPS rating: Moderate

The Great Head Trail is a scenic, short walk that passes largely along cliffs directly above the sea. From the Sand Beach parking area on Park Loop Rd. (user fee required), cross Sand Beach to the east end. Near the seaward end of the interior lagoon, look for a trailhead post and a series of granite steps with a hand rail ascending a high bank. The trail quickly reaches a huge millstone, where the trail turns sharply right (south) switchbacking up the cliff. The path continues to the extremity of the peninsula, then turns northeast along the cliff to the high point, Great Head (145 ft.), where there are ruins of a stone teahouse. The trail descends northwest to a junction at which the right path returns more quickly to the east end of Sand Beach. The path that leads north reaches an abandoned service road in about 0.3 mi. Turn left on the road, and follow it south for about 0.3 mi. to the east side of Sand Beach.

Great Head Trail

Distances from east side of Sand Beach

    to south end of peninsula (via millstone): 0.5 mi., 15 min.

to teahouse ruins: 0.8 mi., 20 min.

to junction with Schooner Head Rd./Sand Beach paths:
   1.3 mi., 35 min.

to start (via service road): 1.6 mi. (2.6 km.), 55 min.

Ocean Trail (also called Shore Path)

NPS rating: Easy

Park at the large, lower Sand Beach parking area on the
Park Loop Rd. From the parking area, follow the asphalt
trail about 50 ft. toward the beach. Where the staircase
descends to the left, turn right to begin the Ocean Trail. As
of publication date, the trailhead was not marked. The trail
leads uphill several hundred yards, crosses through a
small, paved upper parking area, and continues south to
Otter Point, paralleling Park Loop Rd. 1.8 mi. The Ocean
Trail offers spectacular shoreline scenery and follows a
level grade. Of interest en route are Thunder Hole, Monument Cove, and the Otter Cliffs.

Ocean Trail

Distance from Sand Beach
   to Otter Point: 1.8 mi. (2.9 km.), 55 min.

Dorr Mountain (1270 ft./387 m.) Area

Dorr Mountain lies immediately west of Sieur de Monts
Spring. Two routes up the mountain are possible from
Sieur de Monts Spring. Trails also ascend from the north
and south over long ridges. The east and west slopes are
steep. With properly placed cars, a party can have a good
climb leaving from Sieur de Monts Spring, traversing
Dorr, and continuing west to the summit of Cadillac
Mountain (1530 ft.). The route descends to about 1000 ft.

between the 2 summits. There is hiker parking both at the nearby Tarn and on Cadillac's summit. (Hikers are encouraged not to park at the very congested Sieur de Monts Spring parking area. There is a connecting path between the Tarn and the spring parking areas for hikers wishing to visit or begin a hike at the spring.)

Dorr Mountain Trail

NPS rating: Moderate (East Face Trail: Strenuous)

Follow the paved walkway from the Nature Center Parking Area at Sieur de Monts Spring toward the Springhouse. At the rock inscribed Sweet Waters of Acadia, turn right on a walkway that remains paved for a few feet. The trail continues, following a series of switchbacks up the northeast shoulder of Dorr Mountain. The first half has many stone steps. At 0.5 mi., the trail is joined by the Dorr Mountain East Face Trail, entering left, which comes directly up from the north end of the Tarn, a lovely mountain lake. At 1.1 mi. is a junction on the left with a short trail leading to the Dorr Mountain Ladder Trail, which comes directly up from the south end of the Tarn. Much of the next 0.4 mi. to the summit is steep and exposed.

Dorr Mountain Trail
Distances from Sieur de Monts Spring
  to Dorr Mountain East Face Trail junction: 0.5 mi., 30 min.
  to link to Dorr Mountain Ladder Trail: 1.1 mi., 1 hr.
  to Dorr summit: 1.5 mi. (2.4 km.), 1 hr. 20 min.

Dorr Mountain Ladder Trail

NPS rating: Ladder

This trail climbs from the south end of the Tarn up the eastern side of Dorr Mountain. The first half is steep, climbing many stone steps and over iron rungs. At 0.3 mi. the trail bears right to join with the Dorr Mountain Trail. Much of the next 0.4 mi. to the summit is steep and exposed.

Dorr Mountain Ladder Trail
Distance from south end of the Tarn
  to Dorr Summit: 0.6 mi. (1 km.), 50 min.

Dorr Mountain North Ridge Trail
NPS rating: Moderate

This trail begins on the south side of Park Loop Rd. about 1 mi. after the road becomes one-way. It climbs south over the summit of Kebo Mountain (407 ft.), traverses a second hump, and ascends the burned-over ledges of the north ridge to reach the summit of Dorr Mountain.

Dorr Mountain North Ridge Trail
Distance from Park Loop Rd.
  to Dorr summit: 1.9 mi. (3.1 km.), 1 hr. 25 min.

Dorr Mountain South Ridge Trail
NPS rating: Moderate

This trail diverges right from the Canon Brook Trail 0.6 mi. from ME 3 at the southern extremity of Dorr Mountain. It rises with moderate grade over rocky ledges and through evergreen forest. Views of Champlain, Cadillac, and the ocean are frequent during the ascent of the south ridge to the summit.

Dorr Mountain South Ridge Trail
Distances from ME 3
  to start (via Canon Brook Trail): 0.6 mi., 20 min.
  to Dorr summit: 1.9 mi. (3.1 km.), 1 hr. 25 min.

Dorr Mountain Notch Trail

NPS rating: Strenuous

This short trail links the summits of Dorr and Cadillac mountains. From the summit of Dorr Mountain, go north on the North Ridge Trail about 0.1 mi. Then turn left (west) on the Dorr Mountain Notch Trail, which drops quickly and in another 0.3 mi. reaches junctions with the Gorge Path and the A. Murray Young Path in the valley between the 2 mountains. Cross these and continue southwest, ascending to reach the summit of Cadillac.

The start of the trail at the summit of Cadillac may be difficult to see. Walk counterclockwise along the paved trail on the summit to the interpretive sign about Bar Harbor. Look for cairns and paint marks on the granite indicating the beginning of the trail leading to the notch. About 0.3 mi. south of the Park Loop Rd., the trail turns left to cross a brook; be careful to avoid an old wood road that goes straight ahead.

Dorr Mountain Notch Trail

Distances from Dorr Summit

to junction with the Gorge and A. Murray Young paths: 0.4 mi., 15 min.

to Cadillac summit: 0.9 mi. (1.4 km.), 40 min.

A. Murray Young Path

NPS rating: Moderate

Ascending the narrow valley between Dorr and Cadillac mountains from the south, this trail leaves the Canon Brook Trail 0.7 mi. west of ME 3. It climbs gradually to the Gorge Path near its junction with the Dorr Mountain Notch Trail. This point affords relatively quick (if strenuous) access to the summit of either mountain.

A. Murray Young Path

Distances from ME 3

> *to* start (via Canon Brook Trail): 0.7 mi., 25 min.
> *to* Dorr Mountain Notch Trail: 1.9 mi., 1 hr.
> *to* Dorr summit (via the Dorr Mt. Notch Trail): 2.3 mi., 1 hr. 20 min.
> *to* Cadillac summit (via the Dorr Mt. Notch Trail): 2.4 mi. (3.9 km.), 1 hr. 25 min.

Jessup Path

NPS rating: Easy

A pleasant, level woodland walk, this path begins on Park Loop Rd. opposite the first road on the left after the beginning of the one-way section of Park Loop Rd. It follows the west margin of Great Meadow, where it may be flooded as a result of beaver activity. The path passes through a mixed forest of hemlock and hardwood to Sieur de Monts Spring at 0.6 mi. Located here are the Abbe Museum, which has displays of ancient Indian culture; the Wild Gardens of Acadia, a formal garden of native plants; and the Nature Center, with a book-sales area and natural history exhibits. The trail terminates 0.3 mi. farther at the north end of the Tarn.

Jessup Path

Distances from Park Loop Rd.

> *to* Sieur de Monts Spring: 0.6 mi., 20 min.
> *to* north end of the Tarn: 0.9 mi. (1.4 km.), 30 min.

The Tarn Trail (Kane Path)

NPS rating: Moderate

This path leads from the north end of the Tarn south to the Canon Brook Trail, and links the Sieur de Monts Spring area to the southern trails of Dorr and Cadillac mountains, while avoiding ME 3. At its start the path runs south, over a rocky talus slope directly along the west side of the Tarn. After reaching the south end of the Tarn, the trail continues south past a beaver pond at 0.5 mi., then gently climbs until its junction with the Canon Brook Trail.

The Tarn Trail
Distance from north end of the Tarn
 to Canon Brook Trail: 1.4 mi. (2.3 km.), 45 min.

Canon Brook Trail
NPS rating: Strenuous

From a pullout on ME 3 about 0.5 mi. south of the south end of the Tarn and about 2 mi. north of Otter Creek Village, the Canon Brook Trail runs west to join the Pond Trail in the valley south of Bubble Pond. It gives access (via the Pond Trail) to the Jordan Pond area, as well as to the trails running north to Dorr and Cadillac mountains.

From the highway, the trail descends west to Otter Creek and intersects the Tarn Trail at 0.3 mi. Turn left (south) at the intersection and follow the Tarn Trail in the valley of Otter Creek. After a brief, sharp rise from the valley, the trail reaches a junction with the Dorr Mountain South Ridge Trail, which diverges right at 0.6 mi. The trail descends to a junction with the A. Murray Young Path, which goes right at 0.7 mi. Then the trail runs steeply westward up the south bank of Canon Brook for about 0.5 mi. At this point, the trail swings away from the brook, passes a beaver pond at 1.3 mi, and ascends to a small pond known as the Featherbed, where it joins the Cadillac Mountain South Ridge Trail and the Pond Trail.

Canon Brook Trail

Distances from ME 3

   to the Tarn Trail junction: 0.3 mi., 10 min.

   to Dorr Mountain South Ridge Trail junction: 0.6 mi., 25 min.

   to A. Murray Young Path junction: 0.7 mi., 30 min.

   to junction with the Cadillac Mountain South Ridge Trail and the Pond Trail: 1.5 mi. (2.4 km.), 1 hr. 5 min.

Cadillac Mountain (1530 ft./466 m.)

This peak is the highest point on the island. There is an automobile road to the summit, which has parking, a small gift shop, and bathrooms. Accessibility by car makes this summit the busiest in the park. Its height offers commanding views.

Trails approach the Cadillac Mountain summit from all four directions. The long South Ridge Trail begins from ME 3 near the NPS Blackwoods Campground. A short connector accesses the trail from the campground. The steep West Face Trail begins at the north end of Bubble Pond. The North Ridge Trail, beginning on Park Loop Rd., can be connected with the Gorge Trail by the Dorr Mountain Notch Trail, which ends on Park Loop Rd. about 0.5 mi. east of the North Ridge trailhead, creating a pleasant loop up and down Cadillac.

Cadillac South Ridge Trail

NPS rating: Moderate

A relatively long hike for Mount Desert Island, this trail starts on the north side of ME 3, about 50 yd. west of the entrance to the NPS Blackwoods Campground (a flat 0.7

mi. connector links the campground to the trailhead). It climbs generally north. At 1.0 mi. a short loop trail on the right leads to Eagle Crag, which has good views to the east and southeast. The loop trail rejoins the main trail in 0.2 mi. After leaving the woods, the South Ridge Trail rises gently over open ledges. It crosses the Canon Brook Trail about 2.3 mi. from ME 3, in a slight col at the Featherbed. Continuing in the open, it passes close to a switchback in the Summit Rd. and ends at the summit parking area.

Cadillac South Ridge Trail

Distances from ME 3

    to junction with the Eagle Crag Spur: 1.0 mi., 40 min.

    to Cadillac summit: 3.5 mi. (5.6 km.), 2 hrs. 30 min.

        (*descending* Cadillac summit to ME 3, subtract 45 min.)

Cadillac West Face Trail

NPS rating: Strenuous

This steep trail, which starts at the north end of Bubble Pond, is the shortest route to the summit. Begin where Park Loop Rd. passes north of Bubble Pond, using the short spur road to reach the pond and trailhead. The trail rises steeply through woods and over open ledges to a junction with the Cadillac Mountain South Ridge Trail 0.5 mi. from the summit. For the summit turn left (north).

Cadillac West Face Trail

Distances from north end of Bubble Pond

    to Cadillac South Ridge Trail junction: 0.9 mi., 1 hr. 5 min.

    to Cadillac summit: 1.4 mi. (2.3 km.), 1 hr. 25 min.

Cadillac North Ridge Trail

NPS rating: Moderate

This trail follows the north ridge of Cadillac, quickly rising through the stunted evergreens onto open ledges. In winter, the North Ridge Trail is often clear of snow when Summit Rd. and trails on the other parts of the mountain are blocked. To reach the trailhead follow Park Loop Rd. south from the Visitor Center. Take the third left turn (about 3 mi.), following the sign for Sand Beach and Park Loop Rd. Park at a paved pull-off on the north side of the road 0.6 mi. beyond the intersection. The trail starts on the south side of the road. It climbs steadily, always keeping to the east of the automobile road, although it closely approaches road switchbacks on two occasions. For much of the distance both sides of the ridge are visible. The views of Bar Harbor, Eagle Lake, Egg Rock, and Dorr Mountain are excellent.

Cadillac North Ridge Trail

Distance from Park Loop Rd.

 to Cadillac summit: *est.* 1.8 mi. (2.9 km.), 1 hr. 30 min.

Gorge Path

NPS rating: Moderate

Follow Park Loop Rd. south from the Visitor Center. Take the third left turn (about 3 mi.), following the sign for Sand Beach and Park Loop Rd. The Gorge Path starts from a gravel pullout on the south side of Park Loop Rd. 0.8 mi. beyond the intersection. The trail rises south up the gorge between Cadillac and Dorr mountains for 1.3 mi. to the narrow notch between the 2 mountains. The trail ends at this notch at junctions with the Dorr Mountain Notch Trail and the A. Murray Young Path.

Gorge Path

Distances from Park Loop Rd.

to Dorr-Cadillac notch: 1.3 mi., 1 hr. 5 min.

to Cadillac summit (via Dorr Mt. Notch Trail): 1.8 mi. (2.9 km.), 1 hr. 35 min. (in reverse direction, Cadillac summit to Park Loop Rd., subtract about 40 min.)

JORDAN POND AND
SOUTHERN TRAILS AREA

Jordan Pond (274 ft.) is a central trailhead to the Eastern side of Mount Desert Island. Located in the valley between Pemetic Mountain on the east and Penobscot and Sargent mountains on the west, the Bubbles to the north, The Triad and Day Mountain to the southeast, and Eliot Mountain and the Thuya Gardens to the southwest, Jordan Pond offers access to all of these places. The view from the Jordan Pond House across the pond to the Bubbles is justifiably famous.

Jordan Pond Shore Trail
NPS rating: Moderate

This circuit around Jordan Pond is level most of the way, but crosses a rocky slope with occasional loose boulders at the pond's northeastern shore. It is 3.3 mi. long; directions here are for traveling the east shore first. Park at the Jordan Pond parking area, located off the west side of Park Loop Rd., about 0.1 mi. north of the Jordan Pond House. Follow the boat-launch road to the south shore of the pond.

When you reach the pond, turn right to start the circuit. The trails listed below all diverge to the right, because the route described is counterclockwise around the lake.

Along the west side of the pond, the trail runs under the sharp Jordan Cliffs and loses the sun early in the day. The trail along the west shore also has many wet spots and exposed tree trunks. An alternative route is a carriage road that runs along the pond uphill from the trail. Use the Deer Brook Trail to reach the carriage road. The circuit is completed at the south end of Jordan Pond.

Jordan Pond Shore Trail

Distances from Jordan Pond parking area

 to Pond Trail (to Canon Brook Trail): 0.1 mi., 5 min.

 to Jordan Pond Carry Trail (to Eagle Lake): 1.0 mi., 30 min.

 to South Bubble Mountain Trail (to gap between North and South Bubble): 1.1 mi., 35 min.

 to Bubble Gap Trail (to Bubble Gap): 1.5 mi., 45 min.

 to Deer Brook Trail (to Penobscot Mountain): 1.6 mi., 50 min.

 to Jordan Pond parking area: 3.3 mi. (5.3 km.), 1 hr. 40 min.

Jordan Stream Trail

NPS rating: Moderate

This walk along the outlet of Jordan Pond passes through pleasant cedar, maple and spruce woods. The trailhead is reached by a short connecting path from the Jordan Pond House. The path essentially parallels a carriage road, which can be hiked for a return trip.

 At 0.7 mi., the trail passes under a cobblestone bridge and continues descending along the stream. The trail takes a sharp left from the stream at 1.3 miles and rises to end at a carriage road at the base of Lookout Ledge, close to Long Pond.

Jordan Stream Trail

Distances from the Jordan Pond House

 to trailhead: 0.1 mi., 5 min.

 to cobblestone bridge: 0.7 mi., 20 min.

 to carriage road: 1.4 mi. (2.3 km.), 45 min.

Jordan Pond Seaside Trail

NPS rating: Easy

The Jordan Pond Seaside Trail offers an easy, level walk between the Jordan Pond House and Seal Harbor. Starting from the south side of the Jordan Pond House, the trail passes through an evergreen forest. After crossing a carriage road at 0.2 mi., the trail continues on a level course to a private driveway just west of Seal Harbor. Follow the driveway south to ME 3 and Seal Harbor. Parking on the southern terminus of the trail is best found at the entrance to the Park Loop Rd. at Seal Harbor.

Jordan Pond Seaside Trail
Distance from the Jordan Pond House
   to Seal Harbor: *est.* 2.0 mi. (3.2 km.), 1 hr.

Asticou Trail

NPS rating: Easy

The Asticou Trail is reached by the short connecting path from the west side of the Jordan Pond House. This trail follows a level course for most of its distance, yet gains some elevation to reach the Asticou Ridge Trail. It provides an important link to Eliot Mountain as well as a potential leg of a loop over Sargent and Penobscot mountains.

Leaving from the trailhead, the trail goes through a mixed forest of birch, maple, white pine, and spruce. At 0.8 mi., the trail crosses a carriage road. At 0.9 mi., it crosses another carriage road. Access to the Amphitheater Trail leaves right (north-northwest) from this second carriage road. Gradually descending from this point, the trail crosses Harbor Brook at 1.1 mi. The Harbor Brook Trail leaves left at this point. The trail then begins to climb up the Asticou Ridge. At 1.5 mi., the Asticou Ridge Trail leaves left, and the trail levels once again. The Asticou Trail follows straight ahead to a junction with the Sargent Mountain South Ridge Trail at 1.8 mi. At 2.0 mi., the trail ends at a private drive. Note: the private drive is not open to the public. It is recommended that hikers turn back or take other trails leading from the Asticou Trail to reach public areas.

Asticou Trail
Distances from the Jordan Pond House
   to start of the Asticou Trail: 0.1 mi., 5 min.
   to junction with the Amphitheater Trail: 0.9 mi., 30 min.
   to junction with the Harbor Brook Trail: 1.1 mi., 35 min.
   to junction with the Asticou Ridge Trail: 1.5 mi., 50 min.
   to junction with the Sargent Mountain South Ridge
      Trail: 1.8 mi., 1 hr.

Asticou Ridge Trail
NPS rating: Moderate

This trail is reached by following the Asticou Trail for 1.5 mi. Traversing a ledgy ridge, this trail climbs over Eliot Mountain, offering views to the south and east of the ocean, Day Mountain, and The Triad. Gradually descending from the summit, the trail reaches a monument to Charles William Eliot, one of the founders of the park, at 0.9 mi. Descending into the woods, the trail reaches a junction with a side trail to ME 3 (0.4 mi. in length). Keeping right, the trail descends into the beautiful Thuva Gardens.

Asticou Ridge Trail
Distance from junction with the Asticou Trail
   to summit of Eliot Mt.: 0.8 mi., 25 min.

to monument: 0.9 mi., 30 min.
to junction with ME 3 spur trail: 1.1 mi., 35 min.
to Thuya Gardens: 1.4 mi. (2.3 km.), 45 min.

Amphitheater Trail
NPS rating: Moderate

The Amphitheater Trail is a spur trail into the basin of Penobscot Mountain. It leaves right from the Asticou Trail and follows a carriage road for 0.5 mi., where it cuts right (north) off the carriage road to follow Little Harbor Brook to the Amphitheater. The Amphitheater is an impressive rim with the longest carriage-road bridge in Acadia National Park.

Amphitheater Trail
Distances from the Jordan Pond House (via Asticou Trail)
to beginning of trail: 0.9 mi., 30 min.
to Little Harbor Brook: *est.* 1.4 mi., 45 min.
to Amphitheater Bridge: *est.* 2.0 mi. (3.2 km.), 1 hr. 5 min.

Harbor Brook Trail
NPS rating: Moderate

The Harbor Brook Trail connects the Asticou Trail with a point on ME 3 between Bracy Cove and Northeast Harbor. Following the brook for its entire length, the trail passes through beautiful cedar groves, as well as mixed forest. At 1.1 mi., a connector to Eliot Mountain and the Asticou Ridge Trail leaves west. The trail ends on ME 3 at 2.0 mi.

Harbor Brook Trail
Distance from the Asticou Trail
to ME 3: 2.0 mi. (3.2 km.), 1 hr.

The Bubbles
(North Bubble 872 ft./266 m.
and South Bubble 766 ft./ 233 m.)

These two finely shaped, almost symmetrical hills rise above the north end of Jordan Pond. Formerly covered with heavy evergreen growth, they were swept by fire in 1947, leaving many open views.

Trails honeycomb the area, and the best access is from the Bubble Rock parking area about 1.1 mi. south of Bubble Pond on the west side of Park Loop Rd. From the parking area, follow the Bubble-Pemetic Trail west for 0.2 mi. to a junction with the Jordan Pond Carry Trail and the North Bubble Trail.

North Bubble Trail
NPS rating: Strenuous

Following the Bubble-Pemetic Trail west from the Bubble Rock parking area, this trail rises sharply for 0.2 mi. to a junction with the South Bubble Mountain Trail and Bubble Gap Trail. From the Bubble-Pemetic Trail, the North Bubble Trail leaves to the right and continues over the North Bubble summit at 0.4 mi. Beyond the summit, the trail descends to reach Eagle Lake at 1.9 mi. (To complete an excellent loop, go right on the Eagle Lake Trail, following the southwest shore to the junction with the Jordan Pond Carry Trail, entering right, which you can follow south back to the start of the North Bubble Trail.)

North Bubble Trail
Distances from the Bubble Rock parking area
   to beginning of the North Bubble Trail (via the Bubble-Pemetic Trail): 0.2 mi., 10 min.

to summit of North Bubble Mountain: 0.6 mi., 20 min.

to Eagle Lake: 1.9 mi., 1 hr.

to complete loop (via the Eagle Lake Trail): *est.* 3.7 mi (6.0 km.), 1 hr. 55 min.

South Bubble Trail

NPS rating: Moderate

From the junction of the Jordan Pond Carry and North Bubble trails, follow the Jordan Pond Carry Trail south for 0.4 mi. to the Jordan Pond Shore Trail. Turn right (north) and follow the Jordan Pond Shore Trail for less than 0.1 mi. to the start of the South Bubble Trail. The South Bubble Trail traverses South Bubble to the gap between South and North Bubble. There, 0.3 mi. from the Jordan Pond Shore Trail, it meets the Bubble Gap Trail in the gap between the two summits.

South Bubble Trail

Distances from the Bubble Rock parking area

to beginning of the South Bubble Trail: 0.5 mi., 15 min.

to summit of the South Bubble Mountain: 0.7 mi., 30 min.

to junction with the Bubble Gap Trail: 0.8 mi. (1.3 km.), 35 min.

Bubble Gap Trail

NPS Rating: Moderate

This trail diverges from the Jordan Pond Shore Trail, about 0.4 mi. north of the South Bubble Trail, near the northern edge of Jordan Pond. The Bubble Gap Trail rises through the gap between North and South Bubble mountains, offering a link between these mountains and the Jordan Pond Shore Trail. Rising through mixed forest, it meets a junction with the South Bubble and North Bubble trails at 0.2 mi.

Bubble Gap Trail
Distance from Jordan Pond Shore Trail:
  to junction with the North and South Bubble Trails: 0.2
    mi. (0.3 km.), 10 min.

Pemetic Mountain (1248 ft./380 m.) **Area**

Pemetic Mountain is located roughly in the center of the eastern district of the island and offers some of Mount Desert Island's best views. Trails up the west side are short and relatively steep, while routes from the north and south are more gradual and wooded. For the trails from the south, climbers park at the Jordan Pond parking area. This will give access to The Triad and Day Mountain as well as Pemetic. From the north, there is parking at Bubble Pond. From the west, parking is located at Bubble Rock, where the Park Loop Rd. crosses the Bubble-Pemetic Trail.

Pemetic Mountain Trail
NPS rating: Strenuous

This trail traverses the length of the mountain north to south. The views of Jordan Pond, the Bubbles, Sargent Mountain, and Eagle Lake are outstanding.

From the north, the trail leaves from the Bubble Pond parking area at the north end of Bubble Pond. It quickly climbs through spruce-fir forest to a junction with the Bubble-Pemetic Trail at 1.1 mi. The trail reaches the summit of Pemetic Mountain at 1.3 mi. There are excellent views of The Triad, Cadillac Mountain, and Jordan Pond from the summit. The trail then descends gradually to a junction with the West Cliff Trail. Go left to continue on the Pemetic Mountain Trail.

Steeply descending after the junction with the West Cliff Trail through delightful mixed forest, the trail meets the Pond Trail at the notch between Pemetic and The Triad. After crossing the Pond Trail, the trail climbs for 0.6 mi. to the summit of The Triad (698 ft.), giving views to the south and west. The trail then descends over ledges to a carriage path at the base of Day Mountain.

Pemetic Mountain Trail
Distances from Bubble Pond parking area

 to Bubble-Pemetic Trail junction: 1.1 mi., 55 min.
 to Pemetic summit: 1.3 mi., 1 hr. 5 min.
 to West Cliff Trail junction: 1.9 mi., 1 hr. 20 min.
 to Pond Trail: 2.2 mi., 1 hr. 30 min.
 to summit of The Triad: 2.8 mi., 2 hrs.
 to carriage road: 3.1 mi. (5 km.), 2 hrs. 10 min.

Bubble-Pemetic Trail
NPS rating: Strenuous

This trail begins at the Bubble Rock parking area, on the west side of Park Loop Rd. about 1.1 mi. south of Bubble Pond.

 The path enters the woods east of Park Loop Rd. and climbs in almost constant cover. Sometimes following a rocky stream bed, the trail ends at a junction with the Pemetic Mountain Trail about 0.1 mi. north of the summit.

Bubble-Pemetic Trail
Distances from Bubble Rock parking area

 to Pemetic Mountain Trail junction: 0.4 mi., 35 min.
 to Pemetic summit (via Pemetic Mountain Trail): 0.5 mi. (0.8 km.), 40 min.

Pond Trail

NPS rating: Moderate

This slightly graded path leaves from the southeast shore of Jordan Pond to the valley south of Bubble Pond, where the Pond Trail meets the west end of the Canon Brook Trail.

The Pond Trail leaves the shore of Jordan Pond, traveling east, and crosses Park Loop Rd. at 0.1 mi. There is a small parking area at this crossing. Continuing through heavy woods and by easy grades, the path swings in the valley between The Triad and Pemetic Mountain. It crosses the Pemetic Mountain Trail at 0.8 mi., continues northeast to cross a carriage road at 1.1 mi. Continuing to climb, the trail joins the Canon Brook Trail and Cadillac South Ridge Trail at the Featherbed, a pond in the col on the south shoulder of Cadillac.

Pond Trail

Distances from Jordan Pond

   to Pemetic Mountain Trail: 0.8 mi., 25 min.

   to carriage road: 1.1 mi., 40 min.

   to the Featherbed: 2.3 mi. (3.7 km.), 1 hr. 35 min.

Pemetic West Cliff Trail

NPS rating: Strenuous

This very steep trail directly links the Pond Trail to the Pemetic Trail just south of the summit of Pemetic Mountain. Leaving from the Pond Trail, the trail quickly ascends through the forest onto a rocky slope. Occasionally, there are views of Jordan Pond from the cliffs. The climb to the summit of Pemetic Mountain along the Pemetic Mountain Trail is gradual.

Pemetic West Cliff Trail
Distances from Pond Trail parking area on Park Loop Rd.
  to beginning of West Cliff Trail: 0.4 mi., 15 min.
  to junction with the Pemetic Mountain Trail: 1.0 mi.
    (1.6 km.), 45 min.

Day Mountain Trail

NPS rating: Moderate

The Day Mountain Trail starts on the north side of ME 3 approximately 1.5 mi. south of the Blackwoods Campground. The parking area is located on the south side of the highway.

The Day Mountain Trail climbs moderately through the forest for its entire length. Periodically crossing carriage roads, the trail offers beautiful views of Hunter's Beach and Seal Harbor from ledges 0.6 mi. from the trailhead. At 0.9 mi., the summit of Day Mountain is reached. (There is a carriage road which also rises to the summit of Day.) Then descending into the forest quickly, the trail reaches another carriage road at 1.4 mi., across from the Pemetic Mountain Trail. (Cross a cobblestone carriage path bridge to reach the trailhead for the Pemetic Mountain Trail.)

Day Mountain Trail
Distances from ME 3
  to summit of Day Mountain: 0.9 mi., 35 min.
  to carriage rd.: 1.4 mi. (2.3 mi.), 50 min.

Triad–Hunter's Brook Trail

NPS rating: Strenuous

This trail begins on the Park Loop Rd. near the southern overpass of ME 3. It follows along Hunter's Brook, passing through a canopy of cedar, maple, and spruce. At 1.25

mi. the trail bears west from the brook and climbs to a carriage road at 1.5 mi. Crossing the carriage road, the trail continues to climb to a junction with the Pemetic Mountain Trail near The Triad. Then the trail descends for 0.3 mi. to end at The Triad Pass Trail.

Triad-Hunter's Brook Trail

Distances from the Park Loop Rd.

   to carriage path: 1.5 mi., 45 min.

   to jct. with the Pemetic Trail: *est.* 2.2 mi., 1 hr. 15 min.

   to Triad Pass Trail: *est.* 2.5 mi. (4.0 km.), 1 hr. 25 min.

Sargent Mountain (1373 ft./418 m.)
Penobscot Mountain (1194 ft./364 m.)

Penobscot Mountain and Sargent Mountain are open summits about 1 mi. apart. Sargent Pond, a pleasant mountain pond, lies between the 2 summits. From the south, the preferred starting point is Jordan Pond parking area. From here, hikers can climb both Penobscot and Sargent without retracing steps. The longer route up Sargent is from St. James Church on ME 3/198 via the Giant Slide Trail.

The outlying territory to the southwest contains an interesting maze of trails and carriage roads around Bald Peak (974 ft.) and Parkman Mountain (941 ft.). Ample parking is available at two areas: one is on the west side of ME 3/198 and about 0.3 mi. north of Upper Hadlock Pond (reservoir, no swimming); and the other, Parkman Mountain parking area, is on the east side of ME 3/198, about 0.5 mi. north of Upper Hadlock Pond. Upper Hadlock Pond is approximately 2.5 mi. south of where ME 3/198 splits from ME 233.

Penobscot Mountain Trail

NPS rating: Strenuous

This trail starts from the west side of Jordan Stream (outlet of Jordan Pond) about 0.1 mi. west of the Jordan Pond House and is reached by a short connecting path starting from the house.

The trail runs west and, after crossing a carriage road, rises abruptly to the south end of Jordan Ridge, about 0.5 mi. from Jordan Pond House. The trail then swings north, climbing gradually over open granite ledges to the summit of Penobscot Mountain, where it terminates at the Sargent Pond Trail.

For Sargent Pond and the summit of Sargent Mountain, go left on the Sargent Pond Trail 0.2 mi. Sargent Pond (at about 1060 ft.) is a delightful spot nestled between Penobscot and Sargent mountains. From the pond, the Sargent Mountain South Ridge Trail offers easy access to the summit.

Penobscot Mountain Trail
Distances from Jordan Pond House
- *to* Penobscot summit: *est.* 1.5 mi., 1 hr. 10 min.
- *to* Sargent Pond (via Sargent Pond Trail): *est.* 1.7 mi., 1 hr. 15 min.
- *to* Sargent Mountain summit (via Sargent Pond and Sargent Mountain South Ridge trails): *est.* 2.5 mi. (4 km.), 1hr. 50 min.

Jordan Cliffs Trail

NPS rating: Ladder

Take the Penobscot Mountain Trail to reach the Jordan Cliffs Trail. This challenging yet scenic trail leaves the

Penobscot Mountain Trail 0.4 mi. west of the Jordan Pond House, just northeast of the junction of the Penobscot Trail and a carriage road. Bearing right soon after crossing the carriage road, the trail to Jordan Cliffs heads north and rises up the east shoulder of Penobscot Mountain in gradual pitches to the cliffs at 0.8 mi. The trail traverses the Jordan Cliffs, via ladders and handrails, to a junction with the Penobscot East Trail. Turn left on the Penobscot East Trail to reach the summit of Penobscot Mountain. While very steep, the trail is spectacular, with views of the Bubbles, Pemetic, and Jordan Pond.

Continuing straight past the East Face Trail, the Jordan Cliffs Trail traverses the cliffs above Jordan Pond to cross the Deer Brook Trail. It ends on the summit of Sargent Mountain.

Jordan Cliffs Trail

Distances from Jordan Pond House

> *to* Jordan Cliffs Trail (via Penobscot Mountain Trail): 0.4 mi., 15 min.
>
> *to* Jordan Cliffs: 1.2 mi., 55 min.
>
> *to* Penobscot summit (via Penobscot East Trail): 1.7 mi., 1 hr. 20 min.
>
> *to* junction with the Deer Brook Trail: *est.* 1.6 mi., 1 hr. 15 min.
>
> *to* summit of Sargent Mountain: *est.* 2.0 mi. (3.2 km.), 1 hr. 30 min.

Deer Brook Trail

NPS rating: Strenuous

This is a steep, quick ascent of 0.8 mi. to Sargent Pond from the Jordan Pond Shore Trail at the north end of Jordan Pond. The route is entirely wooded and follows the

course of Deer Brook. This trail joins the Sargent Pond
Trail in the valley between Sargent and Penobscot.

Deer Brook Trail
Distance from Jordan Pond Shore Trail
   to Sargent Pond Trail junction: 0.8 mi. (1.3 km.), 45 min.

Sargent Mountain South Ridge Trail
NPS rating: Moderate

This trail starts from a carriage road leaving from a man-
sion known as the Brown Mountain Gate Lodge. The trailhead is located about 1 mi. south of Upper Hadlock Pond,
on the east side of ME 3/198. Follow the carriage path
east, always bearing right at junctions for about 0.7 mi.
There, the trail begins on the north side of the carriage
road.

   The Sargent Mountain South Ridge Trail rises over
the wooded shoulder and passes just southeast of the summit of Cedar Swamp Mountain. A spur trail bears left to
the summit. It drops to cross Little Harbor Brook at 1.2 mi.
The trail then leaves the woods and rises sharply 0.4 mi. to
a junction with the Sargent Pond Trail, which comes in
from the right. The trail continues north over open granite
ledges to the summit of Sargent, past junctions to the left
with the Hadlock Brook Trail at 1.8 mi. and the Maple
Spring Trail at 2.1 mi.

Sargent Mountain South Ridge Trail
Distances from the Gate House
   to Sargent Pond Trail: *est.* 0.7 mi., 30 min.
   to Hadlock Brook Trail: *est.* 2.5 mi., 1 hr. 55 min.
   to Maple Spring Trail: *est.* 2.8 mi., 2 hr. 5 min.
   to Sargent summit: *est.* 3.1 mi. (5.0 km.), 2 hr. 15 min.

Giant Slide Trail

NPS rating: Ladder

This trail is the approach to the Sargent Mountain area from the northwest. The trail starts at St. James Church, a small stone chapel located on the east side of ME 198, about 0.3 mi. north of the intersection with ME 3 and 1.1 mi. south of the intersection with ME 233. The trail leads east 0.4 mi. to the Acadia National Park boundary and continues through woods up a gradual slope to a carriage road, at 0.7 mi. The trail turns sharply right (south) and, following Sargent Brook, rises steeply over the tumbled boulders of Giant Slide. At 1.8 mi., the Parkman Mountain Trail diverges right and the Sargent Mountain North Ridge Trail leaves left. The Giant Slide Trail continues through the notch between Parkman Mountain and Gilmore Peak at 2.4 mi. and descends to end at a junction with the Maple Spring Trail at 2.8 mi.

Giant Slide Trail

Distances from the St. James Church on ME 198

> *to* carriage road crossing: 0.7 mi., 25 min.
>
> *to* Parkman Mountain Trail–Sargent Mountain North Ridge Trail junction: 1.8 mi., 1 hr. 10 min.
>
> *to* Maple Spring Trail junction: 2.8 mi. (4.5 km.), 1 hr. 45 min.

Sargent Mountain North Ridge Trail

NPS rating: Moderate

Leaving the Giant Slide Trail 1.8 mi. from ME 198, this trail ascends east and crosses a carriage road at 0.2 mi. Continuing essentially east, it rises over slanting pitches another 0.6 mi. to a sharp right (south) turn. The final 0.4

mi. to the summit of Sargent is over open ledges offering spectacular views.

Sargent Mountain North Ridge Trail
Distance from Giant Slide Trail
   to Sargent summit: 1.2 mi. (1.9 km.), 1 hr.

Hadlock Brook Trail and Maple Spring Trail
NPS rating: Strenuous

These are the principal routes to Sargent Mountain from the west. From the east side of ME 198 just north of Upper Hadlock Pond and opposite the Norumbega Mountain parking area, the Hadlock Brook Trail runs east 0.4 mi. to a junction, where the Maple Spring Trail leaves left and the Hadlock Brook Trail forks right. From here, there is little difference between the two trails. They are basically parallel, wooded, steep, and rugged, and terminate on the Sargent Mountain South Ridge Trail, south of the summit.

Hadlock Brook Trail and Maple Spring Trail
Distances from ME 198
   to junction with the Bald Peak Trail: 0.3 mi., 10 min.
   to Sargent summit (via either route): 2 mi. (3.2 km.), 1 hr. 35 min.

Grandgent Trail
NPS rating: Strenuous

This trail runs between the summit of Sargent Mountain and the Giant Slide Trail. From the summit of Sargent, the trail leaves west and steeply descends into a saddle at the base of Gilmore Peak. After a short climb of 0.2 mi., the trail reaches Gilmore Peak. Then it gradually descends for 0.3 mi. to end at the Giant Slide Trail.

Grandgent Trail

Distances from the summit of Sargent Mountain

to saddle between Gilmore Peak and Sargent Mountain: 0.5 mi., 15 min.

to Gilmore Peak: 0.7 mi., 25 min.

to junction with the Giant Slide Trail: 1.0 mi. (1.6 km.), 35 min.

Parkman Mountain Trail

NPS rating: Moderate

The Parkman Mountain Trail starts out with the Hadlock Brook Trail but soon diverges north (left) to lead 1 mi. through woods and over a series of knobs to the summit of Parkman Mountain. The trail crosses a carriage road three times on the way to the summit. The Bald Peak Trail joins the trail from the right at 0.9 mi. At the summit, a trail that leaves right (east) connects with the Giant Slide Trail in the gap between Parkman Mountain and Gilmore Peak. The Parkman Mountain Trail continues north over open ledges, then through the woods, crossing a carriage road 0.5 mi. beyond the summit. The trail ends 0.2 mi. farther, at the junction of the Giant Slide Trail and the Sargent Mountain North Ridge Trail.

Parkman Mountain Trail

Distances from ME 198

to Parkman summit: 1 mi., 50 min.

to Giant Slide Trail-Sargent Mountain North Ridge Trail junction: 1.7 mi. (2.7 km.), 1 hr. 10 min.

Bald Peak Trail

NPS rating: Moderate

This trail connects the Hadlock Brook Trail to the Parkman Mountain Trail. The trail is reached by following the Hadlock Brook Trail for 0.3 mi. At this point, the Bald Peak Trail leaves left. Gradually climbing through the forest, the trail reaches the open Bald Peak at 0.8 mi. The trail reaches the Parkman Mountain Trail shortly beyond the summit of Bald Peak.

Bald Peak Trail

Distances from ME 198 (via the Hadlock Brook Trail)
   to beginning of Bald Peak Trail: 0.3 mi., 10 min.
   to summit of Bald Peak: 0.8 mi., 30 min.
   to Parkman Mountain Trail: 0.9 mi. (1.5 km.), 35 min.

Norumbega Mountain (852 ft./260 m.)

Norumbega rises just east of Somes Sound. It is most often climbed from the parking area just north of Upper Hadlock Pond (reservoir, no swimming). You can then descend over the longer south ridge to Lower Hadlock Pond (also a reservoir), and from there walk back to the highway. This summit is wooded, but the blueberries on the north slope make it attractive and appealing in season. The trail offers very good views of Somes Sound and the mountains west of the sound. *Note:* This area is honeycombed with abandoned and unoffical paths. Pay careful attention to trail markers and maps.

Norumbega Mountain Trail

NPS rating: Strenuous

This trail leaves the parking lot on the west side of ME 198 about 0.3 mi. north of Upper Hadlock Pond. It ascends quickly and steeply through woods to granite ledges, then swings south to the summit. The trail descends the south ridge through a particularly fine softwood forest to Lower Hadlock Pond. There, it turns north, following the shore of the pond and Hadlock Brook to Upper Hadlock Pond and ME 198.

Norumbega Mountain Trail

Distance from ME 198 north of Upper Hadlock Pond
  to ME 198 at Upper Hadlock Pond outlet: 2.5 mi. (4 km.), 1 hr. 35 min.

WESTERN DISTRICT
(West of Somes Sound)

Acadia Mountain (681 ft./ 208 m.)

Acadia is the only summit on Mount Desert Island with an east-west ridge trail along the top. The views of Somes Sound are noteworthy. Some prefer to climb from the west, dropping down to Somes Sound from the east promontory. Flowing into Somes Sound at the base of the mountain is Man o' War Brook, where nineteenth-century frigates renewed their water supplies, taking advantage of the deep-water anchorage close to the shore.

Acadia Mountain Trail
NPS rating: Strenuous

Parking is located at the Acadia Mountain parking area on the west side of ME 102, 3 mi. south of Somesville and 3 mi. north of Southwest Harbor (please do not block the fire road gates on the east side of ME 102). The Acadia Mountain Trail begins on the east side of ME 102, across the road from the parking area. Go left at the fork 0.1 mi. down the trail.

The trail ascends the west slope, soon leaving woods for open rocks and frequent views. It passes over the highest summit and reaches the east summit, with views of the sound, at about 1 mi. The trail then descends southeast and south very steeply to cross Man o' War Brook. A junction about 50 yd. beyond the stream marks the end of the Acadia Mountain Trail. To return to ME 102 via the fire road, go west (right) at the junction and proceed past trails to St. Sauveur and Valley Cove, which diverge left about 100 yd. east of the stream. Go through a field for 200 yd. to the east end of the Man o' War Brook fire road. Follow the fire road west over gradual grades about 1 mi. back to ME 102, 50 yd. north of the parking area (you will cross the Acadia Mountain Trail shortly before ME 102; turn left onto the trail to reach the parking lot directly).

Acadia Mountain Trail
Distances from ME 102
>   *to* Acadia Mountain, east summit: *est.* 1 mi., 45 min.
>   *to* Man o' War Brook: *est.* 1.5 mi., 1 hr.
>   *to* ME 102: *est.* 2.5 mi. (4 km.), 1 hr. 30 min.

St. Sauveur Mountain (679 ft./207 m.)

This mountain can be climbed from the north via the Man o' War Brook fire road (NPS fire service road from ME 102), from ME 102 on the west, and from the Fernald Cove Rd. on the south. There are good views of Somes Sound from Eagle Cliff, just east of the summit.

St. Sauveur Trail
NPS rating: Moderate

This trail is an easy route to the summit of St. Sauveur Mountain from the north. Follow the Acadia Mountain Trail description to reach the parking lot and trailhead. Start 0.1 mi. down the Acadia Mountain Trail, and go right at the fork.

The path runs south through evergreens and over open slopes, rising contantly for 1 mi. to a junction with the Ledge Trail entering on the right. From there it is 0.3 mi. to the summit, where the St. Sauveur Trail joins the Valley Peak Trail.

St. Sauveur Trail

Distances from ME 102
    to Ledge Trail junction: 1 mi., 40 min.
    to St. Sauveur summit: 1.3 mi. (2.1 km.), 55 min.

Ledge Trail
NPS rating: Moderate

This trail begins at St. Sauveur parking area on the east side of ME 102 about 0.2 mi. north of the entrance road to the NPS swimming facilities at the south end of Echo Lake. The parking area is also about 0.2 mi. south of the access road to the AMC Echo Lake Camp (private).

   The path enters the woods and rises over ledges to its end. It meets the St. Sauveur Trail 0.5 mi. from the highway and about 0.3 mi. northwest of the summit.

Ledge Trail

Distances from ME 102
    to St. Sauveur Trail junction: 0.5 mi., 25 min.
    to St. Sauveur summit: 0.8 mi. (1.3 km.), 40 min.

Valley Peak Trail
NPS rating: Strenuous

This trail leaves the west side of the Valley Cove truck road a few yards north of the parking area at Fernald Cove. It rises steeply northwest through shady woods over Valley Peak (the south shoulder of St. Sauveur Mountain). The trail then skirts the top of Eagle Cliff, with outstanding views of Valley Cove below and the mountains to the east of Somes Sound. On the summit of St. Sauveur, at 0.8 mi., the St. Sauveur Trail merges from the left. The Valley Peak Trail continues fairly steeply down the northeast shoulder of St. Sauveur to end at a junction with the Acadia Mountain Trail near Man o' War Brook and the east terminus of the Man o' War Brook fire road.

Valley Peak Trail
Distances from the Valley Cove truck road
> *to* St. Sauveur summit: 0.8 mi., 45 min.
> *to* Acadia Mountain Trail junction: 1.6 mi. (2.6 km.), 1 hr. 10 min.

Flying Mountain (284 ft./87 m.)

Guarding the entrance to Somes Sound, this low peak offers perhaps the greatest reward on the island for a small effort. A few minutes' climb to the open top gives a fine panorama of the sound, Southwest Harbor, Northeast Harbor, and the islands to the south—the Cranberries, Greening, Sutton, Baker, and Bear.

Flying Mountain Trail
NPS rating: Moderate

This scenic trail over tiny Flying Mountain leaves the east side of the parking area at the Fernald Cove end of the Valley Cove truck road and rises quickly and steeply through spruce woods. At the edge of Valley Cove, the trail follows the shore north over rock slides and under forbidding Eagle Cliff to end at a junction with the Acadia Mountain Trail at Man o' War Brook.

At Valley Cove, the north terminus of the truck road can be located up the bank about 75 yd. south from the water's edge. For an easy return to the Fernald Cove parking area, follow the road south for about 0.5 mi.

Flying Mountain Trail
Distances from Fernald Cove parking area
   to Flying Mountain summit: 0.3 mi., 15 min.
   to Fernald Cove parking area (via truck road from Valley Cove): *est.* 1.2 mi. (1.9 km.), 45 min.
   to Acadia Mountain Trail junction: 1.5 mi. (2.4 km.), 1 hr.

Beech Mountain (839 ft./256 m.)

Beech Mountain lies between Echo Lake and Long Pond (Great Pond on some maps). Its summit is easy to reach from either the Beech Cliff parking area (located at the end of Beech Hill Rd., in the notch between Beech Cliff and Beech Mountain) or the pumping station area at the foot of Long Pond. (see directions p. 121). Beech Mountain can also be climbed on its southwest flank, beginning at the south end of Long Pond. An added attraction near Beech Mountain is the Beech Cliff–Canada Cliff area just to the east of the Beech Cliff parking area. These rugged cliffs offer spectacular views of Echo Lake.

Beech Cliff Trail

NPS Rating: Moderate (Beech Cliff Ladder Trail: Ladder)

This trail offers access to the beautiful vistas at the top of Beech Cliff via both a moderate loop trail and a strenuous ladder trail. The moderate trail starts at the Beech Cliff parking area. To reach this trailhead, follow ME 102 south through Somesville and take Pretty Marsh Rd., the first right after the fire station. Follow Pretty Marsh Rd. west for about 0.5 mi., where the Beech Hill Rd. intersects from the left. Follow Beech Hill Rd. south until it ends at the parking area.

   The loop trail leaves east and rises moderately to a junction with the Canada Cliff Trail, entering right. To the left here is a short loop along Beech Cliff, with excellent views of Echo Lake, the ocean, and islands to the south.

The Beech Cliff ladder trail (not recommended for those uneasy about heights) begins east of Beech Cliff, at the parking lot for the Echo Lake swimming area. It climbs quickly via ladders to the junction of the Canada Ridge Trail and the Beech Cliff loop.

Beech Cliff Trail

Moderate loop: distance from the Beech Cliff parking area
0.6 mi. (0.8 km.), 30 min.

Ladder trail: distance from the Echo Lake parking area
0.5 mi. (0.8 km.), 40 min.

Canada Cliff Trail

NPS rating: Moderate

This trail, which in portions is also called the Canada Ridge Trail, leaves east from the Valley Trail 0.2 mi. south of the Beech Cliff parking area. It rises east, then turns left at a junction to reach the Beech Cliff Trail. A right turn at the junction leads to a loop trail that runs along Canada Cliff, then rejoins the main trail to Beech Cliff.

Canada Cliff Trail

Distance from Beech Cliff parking area
to Beech Cliff Trail: 0.9 mi. (1.5 km.), 45 min.

Beech Mountain Trail

NPS rating: Moderate

The trail leaves the northwest side of the Beech Cliff parking area and forks in 0.1 mi. The trail to the right (northwest) is 1 mi. long and provides a beautiful vista of Long Pond before climbing to the summit. The trail to the left (south) is 0.6 mi. long and climbs more steeply to the summit of Beech Mountain, with its firetower. The two trails can be combined to form a scenic loop hike.

From the summit, the Beech Mountain West Ridge and South Ridge Trails depart to the southwest and south.

Beech Mountain Trail
Distances from Beech Cliff parking area

to Beech Mountain summit (via north fork): 1.1 mi., 45 min.

to Beech Cliff parking area: (via north fork then south fork) 1.8 mi. (2.9 km.), 1 hr. 15 min.

Valley Trail
NPS rating: Moderate

This graded path is a convenient link between the Long Pond area and the Beech Cliff parking area. It also permits a circuit or one-way trip over Beech Mountain, since it provides direct access to the South Ridge Trail.

The trail enters the woods on the east (right) side of the service road that skirts the east shore of the south end of Long Pond. The entrance is about 0.3 mi. north of the junction with the road to the pumping station. (Or, park at the pumping station. Take the trail east, go right at a fork in 40 or 50 yd. and cross the service road in about 0.3 mi.)

By easy grades over wooded slopes, the trail runs north briefly and then swings east (right) before entering a series of switchbacks on the south slopes of Beech Mountain. At about 0.3 mi., the South Ridge Trail to Beech Mountain leaves left. Continuing east the Valley Trail soon swings north to maintain altitude as it runs up the valley separating Beech Mountain and Canada Cliff. At about 1 mi., there are the remains of the old road to Southwest Harbor and the Canada Cliff Trail comes in from the right. Continue directly ahead (north) 0.2 mi. to the Beech Cliff parking area.

Valley Trail

Distances from service road at Great Pond
  to Beech Mountain South Ridge Trail junction: 0.3 mi.,
    10 min.
  to Old Southwest Harbor Rd. and Canada Cliff Trail
    junction: 1 mi., 40 min.
  to Beech Cliff parking area: 1.2 mi. (1.9 km.), 50 min.

Beech Mountain South Ridge Trail

NPS rating: Moderate

This well-marked trail diverges left from the Valley Trail
about 0.3 mi. east of the service road and steadily ascends
the south ridge to the summit along open ledges, offering
views to the south.

Beech Mountain South Ridge Trail

Distances from service road at Long Pond
  to start (via Valley Trail): 0.3 mi., 10 min.
  to summit of Beech Mountain: 0.9 mi. (1.5 km.), 45 min.

Beech Mountain West Ridge Trail

NPS rating: Moderate

Leaving from the east side of the Long Pond pumping station, this trail skirts the edge of Long Pond for 0.3 mi. At
this point the trail begins to climb from the shore. Rising
steeply at times, there are ledges which offer good views
of the pond and Mansell Mountain. It reaches the Beech
Mountain Loop Trail at 0.9 mi.

Beech Mountain West Ridge Trail

Distances from pumping station
  to junction with the Beech Mountain Loop Trail: 0.9
    mi., 40 min.
  to summit of Beech Mountain (via the Loop Trail): 1.0
    mi. (1.6 km.), 45 min.

WESTERN MOUNTAINS

Bernard Mountain (1071 ft./326 m.)
Mansell Mountain (949 ft./289 m.)

This area has two main summits: Bernard to the west and Mansell to the east. Both summits are wooded, and extensive views are rare. There is access from the north via the Western Trail into Great Notch. From the south, there are many choices: Long Pond Trail, Perpendicular Trail, Sluiceway Trail, South Face Trail, Razorback Trail, and the Cold Brook Trail. You can reach all of the southern approaches from the parking area at the foot of Long Pond near the pumping station. To reach the pumping station, follow Seal Cove Rd. west from Southwest Harbor. Take the first right (toward the landfill) and follow this road until it ends at the pumping station.

Western Trail
NPS rating: Moderate

This is the only trail providing access to the western mountains from the north. There are no open vistas. To reach the trailhead, go about 1 mi. east from the western loop of ME 102 on the Long Pond (sometimes called Great Pond) fire road. Parking is available here. The fire road crosses ME 102 just north of Seal Cove Pond. The Western Trail starts on the southeast side of the road about 0.1 mi. beyond the Pine Hill turnaround and parking area.

The trail trends southeast and rises by easy grades to a junction with the Long Pond Trail (entering left) 1.9 mi. from the fire road. It ends in Great Notch at 2.3 mi. The Great Notch gives access to both western mountain peaks.

Western Trail
Distances from Great Pond fire road
> *to* Long Pond Trail junction: 1.9 mi., 1 hr. 5 min.
> *to* Great Notch: 2.3 mi. (3.7 km.), 1 hr. 25 min.

Long Pond (Great Pond) Trail
NPS rating: Easy

This excellent footpath starts at the pumping station at the foot of Long Pond (sometimes called Great Pond). It follows the west shore of the pond for 1.5 mi., then bears west away from it. Turning south, the trail passes through a beautiful birch forest and follows Great Brook to a junction with the Western Trail. With this route to the Western Trail, you can reach the complex of trails on Bernard and Mansell and complete a circuit back to the pumping station.

Long Pond Trail
Distances from pumping station
> *to* junction with Perpendicular Trail: 0.2 mi., 5 min.
> *to* Western Trail junction: 2.9 mi. (4.7 km.), 1 hr. 40 min.

Perpendicular Trail
NPS rating: Strenuous

This trail, ascending Mansell Mountain, leaves left from the Long Pond Trail on the west shore of Long Pond, 0.2 mi. north of the pumping station. It follows a steep course up the east slope of Mansell, crossing a rock slide. The trail is very steep, much of it passing over stone steps. There are a few iron rungs and one iron ladder along the course of the trail. The upper portion has an excellent view southeast. At an open ledge near the top, watch for a sign marked Path, where an abrupt turn left leads down sharply

and marsh before the trail goes up to the actual summit. The summit is wooded.

Perpendicular Trail

Distances from pumping station
   to start (via Long Pond Trail): 0.2 mi., 5 min.
   to Mansell summit: 1.2 mi. (2.6 km.), 1 hr. 10 min.

Sluiceway Trail

NPS rating: Strenuous

This trail starts at Mill Field on the western-mountain fire road. To reach Mill Field, follow Seal Cove Rd. west from ME 102 in Southwest Harbor. The pavement ends at the Acadia Park border. Take the first right off the dirt road, bear right at the first fork, and left at the second fork. The road ends at Mill Field. The trail runs north 0.6 mi. to a junction with the Great Notch Trail. At this junction, the Sluiceway Trail swings northwest and climbs rather steeply, to a junction with the South Face Trail 0.4 mi. farther. To reach Bernard Peak, follow the South Face Trail left (south) for 0.2 mi.

Sluiceway Trail

Distances from western-mountain fire road
   to Great Notch Trail junction: 0.6 mi., 25 min.
   to South Face Trail junction: 1 mi., 50 min.
   to Bernard summit (via South Face Trail): 1.1 mi. (1.8 km.), 1 hr.

Bernard Mountain South Face Trail

NPS rating: Strenuous

This trail also starts at Mill Field on the western-mountain fire road. (For directions to Mill Field, see the Sluiceway

Trail description.) As do many of the trails on the western mountains, it runs through a magnificent spruce-fir forest and affords fine views of western Mount Desert Island and Blue Hill Bay. It leads west 0.5 mi. and then rises north to Bernard Peak at 1.7 mi. and ends in Little Notch at the junction with the Sluiceway Trail 0.2 mi. beyond.

Bernard Mountain South Face Trail
Distances from western-mountain fire road
> *to* Bernard summit: 1.7 mi., 1 hr. 20 min.
> *to* Little Notch: 1.9 mi. (3.1 km.), 1 hr. 25 min.

Razorback Trail
NPS rating: Strenuous

The Razorback Trail leaves from the Great Notch Trail, which in turn begins at Gilley Field. To reach Gilley Field, follow Seal Cove Rd. west from ME 102 in Southwest Harbor. The pavement ends at the Acadia Park border. Take the first right off the dirt road, bear right at the first fork, and right at the second fork. The road ends at Gilley Field. Follow the Great Notch Trail for 0.2 mi., where the Razorback Trail bears right.

This hike moderately climbs the western side of Mansell, offering views of the Great Notch and Bernard. The trail climbs over ledges and through softwood forest, to connect with the Mansell Mountain Trail between the summit and Great Notch.

Razorback Trail
Distances from Gilley Field
> *to* start of Razorback Trail (via Great Notch Trail): 0.2 mi., 5 min.
> *to* junction with Mansell Peak Trail: 0.9 mi. (1.5 km.), 35 min.

Cold Brook Trail

NPS rating: Easy

This trail is an important link between the Long Pond pumping station trailhead and the western mountains. Running between the Long Pond Trail and Gilley Field, this trail is an easy hike, following the lowlands around Mansell Mountain. It provides access to the Mansell Mountain Trail. More importantly, it is a natural beginning or finish to a circuit hike over both Mansell and Bernard and is a lovely woodlands walk.

Cold Brook Trail

Distances from pumping station
   to start of trail: 0.1 mi., 5 min.
   to Gilley Field: 0.4 mi. (0.6 km.), 20 min.

Great Notch Trail

NPS rating: Moderate

This trail, leaving from Gilley Field, offers a pleasant walk through the notch separating Bernard and Mansell mountains. Gradually rising from the trailhead, the Great Notch Trail provides access to the Razorback Trail, Knight's Nubble, the Little Notch, and the summits of Bernard and Mansell.

Great Notch Trail

Distances from Gilley Field
   to Razorback Trail junction: 0.1 mi., 5 min.
   to Great Notch: 1.1 mi. (1.8 km.), 45 min.

Mansell Mountain Trail

NPS Rating: Moderate

This trail leaves from Gilley Field and offers a beautiful hike up Mansell Mountain. Gradually climbing from the trailhead, this trail passes through softwood forest. It conto climb onto ledges, giving views to the east and south of Southwest Harbor, Beech Mountain, Long Pond, and Northeast Harbor. It meets the Perpendicular Trail at the summit of Mansell.

Mansell Mountain Trail
Distances from Gilley Field
   to outlook spur trail: 0.7 mi., 30 min.
   to Mansell summit: 0.8 mi. (1.3 km.), 35 min.

ISLE AU HAUT

This island, about 5 mi. south of Stonington, was an early landmark for sailors. Samuel de Champlain, a seventeenth-century French explorer, named it High Island. A range of mountains extends for 6 mi., the length of the island. Mount Champlain (543 ft.), near the north end, is its highest summit. Farther south along the ridge are Rocky Mountain (500 ft.), Sawyer Mountain (480 ft.), and Jerusalem Mountain (440 ft.). Near the southwest tip is Duck Harbor Mountain (314 ft.).

The island is reached by mail boat from Stonington (45 min.). The schedule should be checked locally.

About half of the island is within Acadia National Park. The NPS maintains a camping area at Duck Harbor, on the southwest side of the island and about 5 mi. from Isle au Haut Village. There are five lean-to's (no tent sites), which are available by reservation only. The NPS has established daily limits on the number of people allowed to visit Isle au Haut. For the latest information and reservations (available no earlier than April 1 for the following calendar year), call the park headquarters on Mount Desert Island (207-288-3338), or write to Acadia National Park, PO Box 177, Bar Harbor ME 04609.

The 12-mi. road around the island is partly paved. Some sections of the road, however, are very rough and not recommended for bike riding. The road passes the foot of Long Pond, where there is a place to swim.

Numerous trails offer opportunities to explore wild and rocky shoreline, heavily wooded uplands, marshes, and mountain summits. For current hiking information, write to Acadia National Park, stop at the park visitor center in Hulls Cove, or pick up a map from the mail-boat operators. From June to September, park rangers will meet the mail boat and provide you with detailed hiking information.

Goat Trail
NPS rating: Moderate

This trail runs from the southern portion of the main road to the Western Head Rd. It parallels the shoreline and offers spectacular views of Head Harbor, Merchant Cove, Barred Harbor, Squeaker Cove and Deep Cove.

The trail begins in a marshy lowland and gradually rises to the coastal ridge. Passing through an evergreen forest, at 0.6 mi. the trail emerges into a rocky beach. Shortly thereafter, the trail climbs again and passes the southern terminus of the Median Ridge Trail (0.9 mi.). Once again, the trail passes intermittently through both beaches and highlands offering a variety of perspectives on the southern coast of Isle au Haut.

Goat Trail

Distances from main road
   to junction with Median Ridge Trail: 0.9 mi., 30 min.
   to junction with Duck Harbor Mountain Trail: 1.8 mi., 1 hr.
   to junction with Western Head Rd.: 2.2 mi. (3.5 km.), 1
      hr. 15 min.

Cliff Trail
NPS rating: Moderate

This trail leaves from the Western Head Rd. It offers the shortest possible route to the Western Ear, which is a small island accessible only during low tide. It begins by climbing steeply (50 ft.) to reach the coastal ridge. Then, it follows the ridge, passing through an evergreen forest. At 0.6 mi. the trail passes through a rocky beach, offering views of Deep Cove and the coast.

Cliff Trail
Distances from Western Head Road
   to junction with Western Head Trail: 0.7 mi., 40 min.
   to Western Ear: 0.8 mi. (1.3 km.), 45 min.

Western Head Trail
NPS rating: Moderate
This trail follows the western shore of Western Head. It offers spectacular views of the ocean from oceanside cliffs. Included in these views are rock outcroppings in the Western Bay. Combined with the Cliff Trail, the Western Head Trail offers a very nice loop around Western Head. The trailheads are a short walk apart on the Western Head Road.

   The trail begins in lowlands. At 0.2 mi., it begins to gradually climb to a shoreline ridge. Shortly thereafter, it crosses an active stream. While continuing to ascend through an evergreen forest upon a ledge, views of the coast are evident to the west. At 0.4 mi., the trail descends onto a rocky beach. The terrain continues to follow along the coast, ascending and descending between ridge and beach.

Western Head Trail
Distances from Western Head Rd.
   to view of rock outcroppings in the Western Bay: 0.7 mi., 45 min.
   to cliffs: 1.2 mi., 1 hr.
   to junction with Cliff Trail: 1.6 mi. (2.6 km.), 1 hr. 15 min.

Duck Harbor Trail

NPS rating: Moderate

This trail begins at the park ranger station on the north end of the island. As a major connector, this trail offers hiking access to Duck Harbor, Moore's Harbor, Eli Creek, the Bowditch Trail, the Nat Merchant Trail, and the park campground.

Following the marshy lowlands, this trail passes through mature stands of softwoods. At 0.9 mi., a small pond will appear to the left. At 1.5 mi., the Bowditch Trail bears to the left. Shortly thereafter, another junction with the town road cuts off to the right. The trail crosses a sandy beach at 1.9 mi., offering views of the western coast. At 2.2 mi., a park service cabin will be visible. A small side trail which offers views of Deep Cove bears off to the right at 2.7 mi. After crossing the road, the trail offers outstanding views of the ocean and harbor.

Duck Harbor Trail

Distances from park ranger's station

   to junction with Bowditch Trail: 1.5 mi., 45 min.

   to junction with town road: 1.5 mi., 45 min.

   to park service cabin: 2.3 mi., 1 hr. 10 min.

   to junction with side trail to Deep Cove: 2.7 mi., 1 hr. 20 min.

   to second junction with road: 3.0 mi., 1 hr. 30 min.

   to views of harbor and ocean: 3.7 mi., 1 hr. 50 min.

   to Duck Harbor and road: 3.9 mi. (6.2 km.), 2 hrs.

Duck Harbor Mountain Trail
NPS rating: Strenuous

This trail begins on the Western Head Rd. and is one of the most physically challenging trails on Isle au Haut. It climbs over Duck Harbor Mountain, offering terrific views of the harbor as well as the southern end of the island. The trail begins by rapidly ascending ledges. At 0.2 mi., the trail briefly crests. Then, at 0.3 mi., after a short descent, the trail again ascends steeply. It passes through a mixture of softwood forest and open ledge to the summit of Duck Harbor Mountain.

After the summit, this trail continues along the ridge. It goes over the Puddings, offering more views, and descends rapidly through softwood forest and ledges down to a junction with the Goat Trail.

Duck Harbor Mountain Trail

Distances from Western Head Rd.
   to summit of Duck Harbor Mountain: 0.4 mi., 35 min.
   to junction with Goat Trail: 1.2 mi. (1.9 km.), 1 hr. 30 min.

Median Ridge Trail
NPS rating: Moderate

The trailhead is located on the main road in the southern part of the island. This trail has two spurs, north and south, from this point. The south spur connects quickly (0.3 mi.) with the Goat Trail by following low marshlands. The north spur quickly ascends to the ridge. At 0.3 mi., a blue blaze appears on trees. The trail follows the ridge into a Japanese garden, offering views to the east. At 0.7 mi., excellent views can be seen from a ledge area surrounded by small conifers. The trail then descends into a bog. At 1 mi., it crosses the Nat Merchant Trail. The trail continues through marsh, evergreens, and a cedar bog to a junction with the Long Pond Trail.

Median Ridge Trail

Distances from main road

> *to* junction of south spur with the Goat Trail: 0.3 mi., 25 min.
>
> *to* junction of north spur with the Nat Merchant Trail: 1 mi., 45 min.
>
> *to* junction of north spur with the Long Pond Trail: 1.6 mi. (2.5 km.), 1 hr. 30 min.

Nat Merchant Trail

NPS rating: Moderate

The Nat Merchant trailhead is located on the main road on the western shore of the island. This trail begins by entering low marshlands covered in cedar and pine. It crosses several intermittent streams until it meets with the Median Ridge Trail (0.8 mi.). After this junction, the trail begins to climb gradually. It passes over a boulder field and crests at the top of this field offering fine views. Once this ridge is crested, the trail passes through a softwood forest. The trail ends at the main road on the island's eastern side.

Nat Merchant Trail

Distances from main road

> *to* junction with Median Ridge Trail: 0.8 mi., 25 min.
>
> *to* junction with road: 1.2 mi. (1.9 km.), 45 min.

Long Pond Trail

NPS rating: Strenuous

This trailhead is located on the main road on the western portion of the island. While this trail is relatively flat to begin, once on the loop the change of elevation is quite severe. Despite the difficult climb, this trail offers wonderful views of the largest pond on Isle au Haut, not to mention access to the summit of Bowditch Mountain, the Bowditch Trail, and the Median Ridge Trail. The trail forms a nice loop for a day hike.

Beginning at the road, the trail follows a low, wet area for 0.4 mi., where the trail meets the Median Ridge Trail (entering right) and splits into its 2 legs of the loop. The southern loop follows along an old stream bed for quite some time. At 1.1 mi., the trail passes over the old foundation of a building, follows along a stone wall, and then gradually climbs onto a ridge. At 1.7 mi., you will see Long Pond. The trail follows Long Pond north for a short time, bears west and climbs gradually through evergreens to the summit of Bowditch Mountain. At the summit, the Bowditch Trail enters from the right. The Long Pond Trail continues straight ahead and returns to the junction with the southern leg and the Median Ridge Trail.

Long Pond Trail

Distances from main road

    to junction with the Median Ridge Trail: 0.4 mi., 15 min.

    to foundation of old building: 1.1 mi., 35 min.

    to Long Pond (via south leg): 1.7 mi., 55 min.

    to summit and junction with Bowditch Trail (via south leg): 2.4 mi., 1 hr. 30 min.

    to complete the Long Pond Loop: 3.2 mi. (4.6 km.), 2 hrs.

Bowditch Trail

NPS rating: Moderate

This trail runs between the Duck Harbor Trail and the Median Ridge Trail. It offers spectacular views from Bowditch Mountain.

Beginning from the Duck Harbor Trail, this trail follows low marshlands for its first 0.8 mi., where it crosses an active stream and turns onto an old firebreak. After following the firebreak, the trail begins to climb gradually, offering wonderful views of the ocean to the west. It continues to climb through a softwood forest over wet ledge for 1.1 mi. where it reaches the summit of Bowditch Mountain. At this point, it connects with the Long Pond Trail.

Bowditch Trail

Distances from junction with the Duck Harbor Trail

    to sign marking trail: 1.1 mi., 40 min.

    to ledges with views to the west: 1.6 mi., 1 hr.

    to summit and junction with Median Ridge Trail: 2.0
        mi. (3.2 km.), 1 hr. 30 min.

Eli's Creek Trail

NPS rating: Easy

This short trail connects the Duck Harbor Trail and the main road. It travels along Eli's Creek. To reach the trailhead, follow the main road south from the park ranger station for about 2.25 mi. The trail leaves to the right from the road. Quickly, the trail joins the Duck Harbor Trail.

Eli's Creek Trail

Distances from the Ranger Station

    to trailhead on main road: *est.* 2.25 mi., 1 hr.

    to Duck Harbor Trail: *est.* 2.5 mi., 1 hr. 15 min.

Exploring
Mount Desert Island
by Chris Elfring

BEFORE YOU BEGIN exploring the island, stop at the Acadia National Park Visitor Center off Route 3 near Hulls Cove. Pick up a map and a schedule of events, including guided nature walks, boat trips, and evening slide programs. There's no better place to ask questions about the island.

You're bound to drive the Park Loop Rd. during your stay—it's a wonderful introduction to Acadia National Park, and you really should see some of the park's famous sights, such as Thunder Hole and Sand Beach. If you tour before 10:00 A.M. or between 4:30 P.M. and sunset, you'll avoid many of the midday crowds that are common during the summer.

- Bike or hike on the carriage-road network. Try the Hadlock Pond Loop, a lovely 3.9-mi. circuit that offers a wonderful retreat from the bustle of the main roads, plus good views, a waterfall, and three of Rockefeller's unique, hand-carved stone bridges. Start from the Brown Mountain Gatehouse on Route 198. (Light touring bikes should try the Witch Hole Pond loop.) Please **do not** bike on hiking trails anywhere in the park, and please respect other users and park resources when you ride.

- Get up early and pick fresh blueberries, then treat yourself to blueberry pancakes for breakfast. Nothing is better than fresh Maine blueberries—the tiny, wild ones are far sweeter than the supermarket variety.

- Ship Harbor Nature Trail in Bass Harbor/Southwest Harbor is fun anytime, but especially on those drizzly, foggy Maine days. It's an easy, 1.6-mi. walk over fairly level ground, and the fog imparts a ghostly stillness. Spend some time sitting on the rocks listening. Both this trail and the nearby Wonderland Trail are beautiful, easy family hikes.

- Explore Bar Island at the edge of Frenchman Bay, from which Bar Harbor draws its name. When the tide is low, a gravel bar connects the island to the mainland and you can walk across. Don't forget to walk back before the tide returns and covers the bar, stranding you on the wrong side. You have about 1-1/2 hours on either side of low tide for exploring.

- Hike up Acadia Mountain, a short but strenuous, 2.5-mi. circuit hike. Your reward for the steep grades and steady climbing is an unbelievable view out Somes Sound toward the Cranberry Isles. Try climbing Beech Mountain on the island's west side for another hike with spectacular views.

- Isle au Haut, or High Island, is a secluded, offshore island that few visitors see. This hidden part of Acadia National Park takes some effort to reach—you go by mail boat from Stonington, ME—but offers some unsurpassed day hiking. No bikes are allowed. Schoodic Peninsula, about 45 mi. by car up the coast from Mount Desert Island, is also part of Acadia and offers a scenic loop road.

- Treat yourself and a friend to a lobster dinner, not at a fancy restaurant but from one of the small, roadside stands where you can get dinner "to go." Drive to somewhere scenic along the coast and picnic on the rocky cliffs.

- Take a boat trip to get an ocean-side view of the island. It does cost money, but provides great opportunities for seeing eagles, osprey, seals, and porpoises, and learning about the island's history. You can go out on a lobster boat, tour Frenchman Bay, or visit rugged Baker Island and imagine what life was like for a pioneer family. The view of MDI from Baker Island is spectacular.

- Feeling hot and tired? You can wade in the ocean at Sand Beach, where the water rarely warms up to 60° and few adults have the courage to submerge completely. For a swim, try Echo Lake on the west side of the island.

- An hour or two before sunset, walk to one of the island's many beaver ponds. These animals are active at dusk and through the night; that's when you're most likely to see a small, doglike head swimming fluidly through the water or to hear the sharp splash of one slapping his tail against the water in warning. Bring binoculars and bug repellent. Look for a lodge (a conical mass of twigs and mud), a well-maintained dam, and chewed stumps to indicate an active beaver pond.

- Stop for hot tea and fresh popovers on the lawn of the Jordan Pond House off the Park Loop Road and admire the lovely view of the Bubbles. Stopping here for midday refreshment is a long tradition among island visitors.

- Make a special effort to explore the west side of the island, where it's quieter and less trammeled. Visit Southwest Harbor to view the sleek and expensive sailboats; continue on to Bass Harbor or Bernard to see lobster boats and other working vessels. Everyone stops at Bass Harbor Head to take pictures of the island's only remaining lighthouse. If you have a canoe or kayak, you might try paddling in scenic Pretty Marsh Harbor in the late afternoon or early evening.

- Volunteer a half-day of your time to help maintain Acadia's trails. Ask at the visitor center or park headquarters about how to join volunteer trail crews.

Sources For
More Information

Abrell, Diana F. and Bunny LaDouceur. *A Guide to the Carriage Roads in and near Acadia National Park*. 1986.

Burt, William H. and Richard P. Grossenheider. *A Field Guide to Mammals*. The Peterson Field Guide Series: 1980.

Butcher, Russel D. *Field Guide to Acadia National Park, Maine*. 1977.

Collier, Sargent F. *Mt. Desert Island and Acadia National Park: An Informal History*. 1978.

Conant, Roger. *A Field Guide to Reptiles and Amphibians*. The Peterson Field Guide Series: 1975.

Coulombe, Deborah A. *The Seaside Naturalist: A Guide to Nature Study at the Seashore*. 1984.

Katona, Steven K., Valerie Rough, and David T. Richardson. *A Field Guide to the Whales, Porpoises, and Seals of the Gulf of Maine and Eastern Canada*. 1983.

Marchand, Peter J. *North Woods: An Insider Look at the Nature of Forests in the Northeast*. 1987.

Peterson, Roger Tory and Margaret McKenny. *A Field Guide to Wildflowers*. The Peterson Field Guide Series: 1968.

Peterson, Roger Tory. *A Field Guide to Birds*. The Peterson Field Guide Series: 1947.

Petrides, George A. *A Field Guide to Trees and Shrubs*. The Peterson Field Guide Series: 1972.

Scheid, Margaret. *Discovering Acadia: A Guide for Young Naturalists*. 1987.

Trails

Acadia Mountain Trail **113**
Acadia (Robinson) Mountain...113
Acadia National Park. *see* Mount Desert Island 73
Amphitheater Trail **97**
A. Murray Young Path...**86**
Asticou Ridge Trail **96**
Asticou Trail **95**

Bald Peak, Mount Desert Island...111
Bald Peak Trail, Mount Desert Island..**111**
Beachcroft Trail **79**
Bear Brook Trail (Champlain Mountain).....................................**78**
Beech Cliff 117
Beech Cliff Trail **117**
Beech Mountain 117
Beech Mountain South Ridge Trail **120**
Beech Mountain Trail **118**
Beech Mountain West Ridge Trail **120**
Beehive, the...81
Beehive Trail **80**
Bernard Mountain 121
Bernard Mountain South Face Trail **123**
Bowditch Trail (Isle au Haut)...**134**
Bowl, the..80
Bowl Trail **80**
Bubble Gap Trail...**99**
Bubble-Pemetic Trail **101**
Bubbles, the...98

Cadillac Mountain 89
Cadillac South Ridge Trail **89**
Cadillac North Ridge Trail...**91**
Cadillac West Face Trail **90**
Canada Cliff 118
Canada Cliff Trail **118**

Canada Ridge Trail..**118**
Canon Brook Trail...**88**
Champlain, Mount, Isle au Haut 127
Champlain Mountain, Mount Desert...77
Cliff Trail **128**
Cold Brook Trail **125**

Day Mountain Trail **103**
Deer Brook Trail **106**
Dog (St. Sauveur) Mountain 114
Dorr (Flying Squadron) Mountain 83
Dorr Mountain Ladder Trail **84**
Dorr Mountain North Ridge Trail..**85**
Dorr Mountain Notch Trail...**86**
Dorr Mountain South Ridge Trail..**85**
Dorr Mountain Trail..**84**
Dry (Dorr or Flying Squadron) Mountain.................................83
Duck Harbor Campsite..130
Duck Harbor Mountain Trail (Isle au Haut) **131**
Duck Harbor Trail (Isle au Haut) **130**

Eagle Cliff, St. Sauveur Mountain 114
Eagle Lake Trail **98**
Eastern District...77
Echo Lake..115
Echo Lake Camp 115
Eli's Creek Trail **134**

Featherbed, the 88, 102
Flying Mountain..116
Flying Mountain Trail **116**
Flying Squadron (Dorr) Mountain 83

Giant Slide...108
Giant Slide Trail...**108**
Gilmore Peak, Sargent Mountain 108
Goat Trail (Isle au Haut)..**128**
Gorge Path **91**
Gorham Mountain 77
Gorham Mountain Trail...**81**
Grandgent Trail **109**
Great Head 82
Great Head Trail **82**
Great Notch Trail **125**
Great Pond Trail **122**

Green Mountain. *See* Cadillac Mountain 89
Hadlock Brook Trail...**109**
Harbor Brook Trail...**97**
Huguenot Head..79

Isle au Haut 127

Jerusalem Mountain, Isle au Haut 127
Jessup Path **87**
Jordan Cliffs 106
Jordan Cliffs Trail..**105**
Jordan Pond..93
Jordan Pond Carry Trail 94
Jordan Pond Seaside Trail **95**
Jordan Pond Shore Trail **93**
Jordan Ridge..105
Jordan Stream Trail **94**

Kane Path (Tarn Trail)...**87**
Kebo Mountain..85

Ledge Trail (St. Sauveur Mountain) **115**
Little Notch, Western Mountain 124
Long (Great) Pond Trail..**122**
Long Pond Trail (Isle au Haut)...**133**

Mansell Peak, Western Mountain 122
Mansell Mountain 121
Mansell Mountain Trail...**125**
Maple Spring Trail..**109**
Median Ridge Trail **131**
Mount Desert Island..73
Nat Merchant Trail (Isle au Haut) **132**
North Bubble Trail...**98**
Norumbega Mountain 111
Norumbega Mountain Trail...**111**

Ocean Drive. *See* Park Loop Road..77
Ocean Trail...**83**
Otter Cliffs 83

Park Loop Road, Mount Desert Island..77
Parkman Mountain 104
Parkman Mountain Trail **110**
Pemetic Mountain 100
Pemetic Mountain Trail...**100**

Pemetic West Cliff Trail **102**
Penobscot Mountain 104
Penobscot Mountain Trail **104**
Perpendicular Trail **122**
Pine Hill, Western Mountain 121
Pond Trail **102**
Precipice Trail **77**

Razorback Trail **124**
Rocky Mountain, Isle au Haut 127

St. Sauveur (Dog) Mountain 114
St. Sauveur Trail **114**
Sargent Mountain 104
Sargent Mountain North Ridge Trail **108**
Sargent Mountain South Ridge Trail **107**
Sargent Pond Trail **107**
Sawyer Mountain, Isle au Haut 127
Sieur de Monts Spring...83
Sluiceway Trail **123**
South Bubble Trail **99**
South Face Trail (Western Mountain) **123**

Tarn, the 79
Tarn Trail (Kane Path)...**87**
Thunder Hole 83, 135
Triad, The..100-104
Triad-Hunters Brook Trail **103**

Valley Peak (St. Sauveur Mountain)......................................115
Valley Peak Trail...**115**
Valley Trail (Beech Mountain) **119**

Western District, Acadia National Park 113
Western Head Trail...**129**
Western Mountains 121
Western Trail (Western Mountain)...................................**121**

Young, A. Murray, Path **86**

Nature

Common Coniferous Trees

Eastern white pine (*Pinus strobus*) 15
Red pine (*Pinus resinosa*) 16
Pitch pine (*Pinus rigida*) 17
Red spruce (*Picea rubens*) 17
White spruce (*Picea glauca*) 18
Eastern hemlock (*Tsuga canadensis*) 18
Balsam fir (*Abies balsamea*) 19
Northern white cedar (*Thuja occidentalis*) 20

Common Deciduous Trees

Bigtooth aspen (*Populus grandidentata*) 20
Quaking aspen (*Populus tremuloides*) 21
American beech (*Fagus grandifolia*) 22
White birch (*Betula papyrifera*) 22
Yellow birch (*Betula lutea*) 23
Red maple (*Acer rubrum*) 24
Sugar maple (*Acer saccharum*) 25
Striped maple (*Acer pensylvanicum*) 25
Northern red oak (*Quercus rubra*) 26
Scrub oak (*Quercus ilicifolia*) 26

Forest Wildflowers

Canada dogwood (*Cornus canadensis*) 28
Canada mayflower (wild lily of the valley) (*Maianthemum canadense*) 28
Indian pipe (*Monotropa uniflora*) 29
Painted trillium (*Trillium undulatum*) 29
Solomon's seal (*Polygonatum biflorum*) 30
False solomon's seal (*Smilacina racemosa*) 30
Starflower (*Trientalis borealis*) 30
Trailing arbutus (*Epigaea repens*) 30
Wintergreen (checkerberry) (*Gaultheria procumbens*) 30

Open-Terrain Wildflowers

Beach pea (*Lathyrus japonicus*) 31
Bluet (*Houstonia caerulea*) 31
Fireweed (*Epilobium angustifolium*) 31
Harebell (*Campanula rotundifolia*) 31
Orange hawkweed (*Hieracium aurantiacum*) 32

Ox-eye daisy (*Chrysanthemum leucanthemum*) 32
Queen Anne's lace (wild carrot) (*Daucus carota*)...32
Wild lupine (*Lupinus perennis*) 32
Yarrow (*Achillea millefolium*) 32

Common shrubs

Lowbush blueberry (*Vaccinium angustifolium* and *V. vacillans*) 32
Black huckleberry (*Gaylussacia baccata*) 33
Mountain cranberry (*Vaccinium vitis-idaea*) 33
Small cranberry (*Vaccinium oxycoccus*) 33
Large cranberry (*Vaccinium macrocarpon*) 33
Sheep laurel (*Kalmia angustifolia*) 33
Rhodora (*Rhododendron canadense*)...34
Rugosa rose (*Rosa rugosa*) 34
Staghorn sumac (*Rhus typhina*) 34
Sweet fern (*Comptonia peregrina*) 34
Dwarf juniper (*Juniperus communis*)..35

Other Plants

Bracken fern (*Pteridium aquilinium*) 35
Cinnamon fern (*Osmunda cinnamonea*) 36
Christmas fern (*Polystichum arostichoides*) 35
Interrupted fern (*Osmunda claytoniana*)...36
Hair cap moss (*Polytrichum commune*) 36
Sphagnum mosses (*Sphagnum sps.*) 36
Common reindeer moss (*Cladonia*)..38
British soldiers (*Cladonia cristatella*)..38
Boulder lichen 38
Map lichen 38

Mammals

Little brown bat (*Myotis lucifugus*)..39
Beaver (*Castor canadensis*) 40
Eastern chipmunk (*Tamias striatus*) 41
Coyote (*Canis latrans*)...41
White-tailed deer (*Odocoileus virginianus*)..41
Fox (*Vulpes fulva*)..41
Snowshoe hare (*Lepus americanus*)...42
Raccoon (*Procyon lotor*)..42
Red squirrel (*Tamiasciurus hudsonicus*)..42
Long-tail weasel (*Mustela frenata*)..42

Common Coastal Birds

Bald eagle (*Haliaetus leuocephalus*) 43
Black guillemot (*Cepphus grylle*) 43

Double-crested cormorant (*Phalacrocorax auritus*)..44
Common eider (*Somateria mollissima*) 45
Herring gull (*Larus argentatus*)..45
Great black-backed gull (*Larus marinus*) 46
Great blue heron (*Ardea herodias*) 46
Common loon (*Gavia immer*) 46
Osprey (*Pandion haliaetus*) 48
Semipalmated plover (*Charadrius semipalmatus*)..49
Sanderling (*Calidris alba*)..49
Common tern (*Sterna hirundo*)..49
Greater and lesser yellowlegs (*Tringa melanoleuca* and *Tringa flavipes*) 50

Common Inland Birds
Blackcapped chickadee (*Parus atricapillus*) 50
Peregrine falcon (*Falco peregrinus*) 51
Ruffed grouse (*Bonasa umbellus*)..52
Red-breasted nuthatch (*Sitta canadensis*) 52
Oven bird (*Seiurus aurocapillus*) 52
Raven (*Corvus corax*) 53
White-throated sparrow (*Zonotrichia albicollis*) 53
Scarlet tanager (*Piranga olivacea*)..53
Myrtle warbler (*Dendroica coronata coronata*) 54
Black-throated green warbler (*Dendroica virens*) 54
Cedar waxwing (*Bombycilla cedrorum*) 54
Downy woodpecker (*Dendrocopus pubescens*)..54
Pileated woodpecker (*Hylatomus pileatus*)..54

Reptiles
Eastern garter snake (*Thamnophis sirtalis sirtalis*)..56
Eastern milk snake (*Lampropeltis triangulum triangulum*)..56
Eastern smooth green snake (*Opheodrys nernalis*)..56
Snapping turtle (*Chelydra serpentina*)..56
Eastern painted turtle (*Chrysemys picta picta*) 56

Amphibians
Green frog (*Rana clamitans melanota*)..57
Leopard frog (*Rana pipiens*) 57
Pickerel frog (*Rana palustris*)..57
Wood frog (*Rana sylvatica*) 58
Spring peeper (*Hyla crucifer*) 58
Northern dusky salamander (*Desmognathus fuscus fuscus*) 58
Red-backed salamander (*Plethodon cinereus cinereus*) 58

Insects
Tiger swallowtail butterfly (*Papilio glaucus*) 59

Monarch butterfly (*Danaus plexippus*) 59
Clouded or orange sulphur butterfly (*Colias philodice or Colias eurytheme*) 59
Common blue butterfly (*Lycaenopsis argiolus*) 59
Dragonflies...60
Damselflies..60
Fireflies 60
Cecropia moth (*Nyalaphora cecropia*) 60
Luna moth (*Actias luna*)...60
Polyphemus moth (*Antheraea polyphemus*) 60
Waterboatman 60
Water striders 60

Common Seaweeds

Corallina (*Corallina officinalis*)...62
Dulse (*Rhodymeria palmata*) 63
Irish moss (*Chondrus crispus*) 63
Kelps 63
Laver (*Porphyra sps.*) 63
Sea lettuce (*Ulva lactuca*) 63
Bladder wrack (*Fucus vesiculosis*)...63
Knotted wrack (*Ascophyllum nodosum*) 63

Common Tidepool Animals

Rock barnacle (*Balanus balanoides*) 64
Green crab (*Carcinus maenas*)..65
Hermit crab (*Pagurus acadianus*)..65
Rock crab (*Cancer irroratus*)...65
Limpet (*Acmaea sps.*)..66
American lobster (*Homarus americanus*) 66
Blue mussel (*Mytilus edulis*)..66
Common periwinkle (*Littorina litorea*) 66
Sea cucumber (*Cucumaria frondosa*)..67
Blood star (*Henricia sanguinolenta*)..67
Daisy brittle star (*Ophiopholis aculeaata*)..68
Purple sea star (*Asterias vulgaris*)...68
Green sea urchin (*Strongylocentrotus droebachiensis*) 68
Dog whelk (*Thais lapillus*)..69

Marine Mammals

Gray seal (*Halichoerus grypus*) 69
Harbor seal (*Phoca vitulina concolor*) 70
Harbor porpoise (*Phocoena phocoena*) 71
Finback whale (*Balaenoptera physalus*) 72
Minke whale (*Balaenoptera acutorostrata*)...72
Humpback whale (*Megaptera novaeangliae*).......................................72

About the AMC

THE APPALACHIAN MOUNTAIN CLUB pursues a vigorous conservation agenda while encouraging responsible recreation, based on the philosophy that succcessful, long-term conservation depends upon firsthand experience of the natural environment. Fifty-four thousand members have joined the AMC to pursue their interests in hiking, canoeing, skiing, walking, rock climbing, bicycling, camping, kayaking, and backpacking, and—at the same time—to help safeguard the environment in which these activities are possible.

Since it was founded in 1876, the Club has been at the forefront of the environmental protection movement. By cofounding several of New England's leading environmental organizations, and working in coalition with these and many more groups, the AMC has positively influenced legislation and public opinion.

Volunteers in each chapter lead hundreds of outdoor activities and excursions and offer introductory instruction in backcountry sports. The AMC education department offers members and the public a wide range of workshops, from introductory camping to the intensive Mountain Leadership School taught on the trails of the White Mountains.

The most recent efforts in the AMC conservation program include river protection, Northern Forest Lands policy, Sterling Forest (NY) preservation, and support for the Clean Air Act.

The AMC's research department focuses on the forces affecting the ecosystem, including ozone levels, acid rain and fog, climate change, rare flora and habitat protection, and air quality and visibility.

AMC Trails

The AMC trails program maintains over 1,400 miles of trail (including 350 miles of the Appalachian Trail) and more than 50 shelters in the Northeast. Through a coordinated effort of volunteers, seasonal crews, and program staff, the AMC contributes more than 10,000 hours of public service work each summer in the area from Washington, D.C. to Maine.

In addition to supporting our work by becoming an AMC member, hikers can donate time as volunteers. The club offers four unique weekly volunteer base camps in New Hampshire, Maine, Massachusetts, and New York. We also sponsor ten-day service projects throughout the United States, Adopt-a-Trail programs, trails day events, trail skills workshops, and chapter and camp volunteer projects.

The AMC has a longstanding connection to Acadia National Park. Working in cooperation with the National Park Service and Friends of Acadia, the AMC Trails Program provides many opportunities to preserve the park's resources. These include half-day volunteer projects for guests at AMC's Echo Lake Camp, ten-day service projects, weeklong volunteer crews in the fall, and trails day events. For more information on these public service volunteer opportunities, contact the AMC Trails Program, Pinkham Notch Visitor Center, P.O. Box 298, Gorham NH 03581; 603-466-2721.

Begin a New Adventure—Join the AMC

We invite you to join the Appalachian Mountain Club and share the benefits of membership. Every member receives *AMC Outdoors*, the membership magazine that, ten times a year, brings you not only news about environmental issues and AMC projects, but also listings of outdoor activities, workshops, excursions, and volunteer opportunities. Members also enjoy discounts on AMC books, maps, educational workshops, and guided hikes, as well as reduced fees at all AMC huts and lodges in Massachusetts and New Hampshire.

To join, send a check for $40 for an adult membership, or $65 for a family membership to AMC, Dept. S7, 5 Joy Street, Boston MA 02108; or call 617-523-0636 for payment by Visa or MasterCard.   S7